Spiralize now!

DENISE SMART

weldon**owen**

weldon**owen**

Published in North America by Weldon Owen, Inc.
1045 Sansome Street, San Francisco, CA 94111
www.weldonowen.com

Weldon Owen is a division of **BONNIER**

First published in Great Britain in 2015 by
Hamlyn, a division of Octopus Publishing

Library of Congress Cataloging-in-Publication data is available

ISBN-13: 9781681880518
ISBN-10: 1681880512

Printed and bound in China

This edition printed in 2015
10 9 8 7 6 5 4 3 2 1

Both imperial and metric measurements have been given
in all recipes. Use one set of measurements only and not
a mixture of both.

Standard level spoon measurement are used in all recipes.
1 tablespoon = one 15 ml spoon
1 teaspoon = one 5 ml spoon

Eggs should be large, butter should be unsalted and fresh
herbs should be used unless otherwise stated.

~contents~

it's time to get spiralizing 4

light bites 8

salads 32

mains 50

sides and extras 84

sweet treats 104

index 126

acknowledgments 128

it's time to get spiralizing

The benefits of spiralizing

A spiralizer is an affordable, easy-to-use cutting machine with a selection of blades that you can use to create a variety of different noodles and ribbons from vegetables and fruit. It's the ideal gadget for health-conscious cooks, as it can help you to cut back on refined carbohydrates, such as pasta and rice, by replacing them with spiralized fruit and vegetables so that you can enjoy your meals while eating fewer calories. A spiralizer will also encourage you to include more fruit and vegetables in your diet and can be a life-saver for those following special diets, such as low-carb, gluten-free and raw food.

Spiralizing can also help you to save time, as it's really quick and easy to prepare fruit and vegetables using the tool. And spiralizing can also reduce cooking times because many of the vegetables and fruit prepared in this way can be eaten raw or just cooked very lightly, which helps retain nutrients.

Choosing a spiralizer

There are many brands on the market, but all essentially work in the same way. The larger horizontal and vertical ones are better for heavier root vegetables and everyday use, but small hand-held ones are ideal if you are cooking for one or for occasional use.

Spiralizers usually come with several different blades, each of which creates a different shape. For this book, I used a horizontal spiralizer with three blades, which I have called the 3 mm (⅛ inch) spaghetti blade, the 6 mm (¼ inch) flat noodle blade and the ribbon blade.

3 mm (⅛ inch)
spaghetti blade

6 mm (¼ inch)
flat noodle blade

Ribbon blade

How to use a horizontal spiralizer

1 Attach the machine to the work surface using the suction feet or lever.

2 Insert the blade you wish to use into the machine.

3 Prepare the fruit or vegetable according to the recipe: peel it, if called for, trim off ends to make a flat surface and cut in half crosswise, if necessary.

4 Attach one end of the prepared fruit or vegetable to the blade and then clamp the other end of the vegetable to the spiky grip on the crank handle.

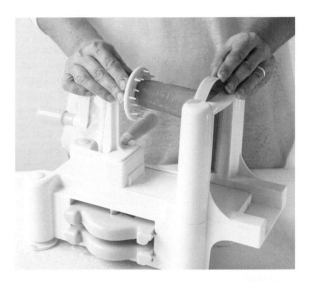

5 Grasp the side handle for leverage, turn the crank handle and apply a little pressure so that the fruit or vegetable is pressed between the blade and the handle – this will create spirals.

6 Finally, remove the long core and a round disc that remains at the end of the spiralizing process.

Tips for successful spiralizing

• Choose firm fruit and vegetables without pits, seeds or hollow centers: the only exceptions are butternut squash (just use the non-bulbous end) and green papaya.

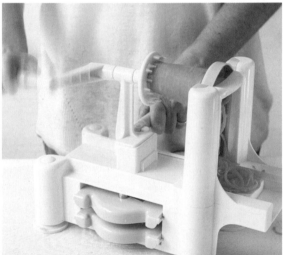

• Vegetables and fruit should not be soft or juicy – pineapples, melons and eggplants will fall apart when you spiralize them.

• Choose vegetables that are as straight as possible. Occasionally you may have to re-center the vegetables to avoid half moon shapes.

• Make sure the ends of fruit and vegetables are as flat as possible by slicing a small piece off either end. Uneven ends can make it difficult to secure the fruit or vegetable to the spiralizer and may cause them dislodge or misalign.

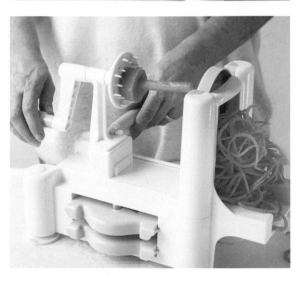

• If you find that a fruit or vegetable is not spiralizing very well, it may be because there is not a large enough surface area for the spiralizer to grip to. For best results, lengths should be no longer than 5 inches (12 cm) and about 1½ inches (3.5 cm) in diameter. Cut any large vegetables in half crosswise.

it's time to get spiralizing

Vertical spiralizer

Horizontal spiralizer

Hand-held spiralizer

• You will be left with a long core and a round disk at the end of the spiralizing process. Save these cores to use when making soups or for snacks.

• A lot of juice is squeezed out of fruit and vegetables when you spiralize them, especially from zucchini, carrots, cucumber, potatoes, apples and pears. Just pat the spirals dry on paper towels before use.

• Be careful when cleaning your spiralizer, as the blades are very sharp. Wash the machine in hot soapy water and use a small kitchen brush or toothbrush to remove stubborn bits of fruit or vegetables from the blades.

Which fruit and vegetables can be spiralized?
I tested many different types of fruit and vegetables while writing and testing the recipes for this book. To save you wasting precious fruit and vegetables, here is a list of the ones that I found to work best.

Apples There's no need to peel or core apples, just trim the ends and spiralize whole – the core is left behind in the machine. Spiralized apples are perfect for use in

salads and savory dishes as well as desserts. Remember that the spiralized apple will turn brown very quickly, so use immediately or dress with lemon juice.

Beets There's no need to peel fresh beets, just wash the skin, flatten the ends and spiralize whole. Eat raw in salads or bake into delicious beet crisps.

Broccoli Don't throw away broccoli stems when you cook broccoli – the stems spiralize really well. For best results, stir-fry or steam the spiralized broccoli stems.

Butternut squash To avoid the seeds, you should only use the non-bulbous end of the squash. Snip any really long strands of spiralized squash into smaller pieces using scissors – this will make the squash easier to eat.

Carrots Choose large carrots for spiralizing. Eat spiralized carrots raw in salads or steam carrot ribbons to create a delicious accompaniment.

Celery root The best way to prepare this root vegetable is to use a sharp knife to remove the knobby brown skin from the celery root and then peel it, cut it in half crosswise and trim to make the ends flat. Spiralized celery root works well in gratins, soups and salads.

Cucumbers Once you've spiralized the cucumber you just need to pat the spirals or ribbons dry. Cucumbers make beautiful ribbons for use in salads.

Daikon Spiralized daikon makes a great alternative to rice noodles.

Green papaya You can find green papaya in Asian supermarkets. Although it is hollow, it attaches to the spiralizer well. Perfect eaten raw in salads.

Green plantains Choose plantains that are as straight as possible and remove the tough outer green skin. Spiralized green plantain is delicious in curries.

Jerusalem artichokes Choose large vegetables. There's no need to peel these knobby vegetables, all you need to do is wash them. If you're not using the spiralized vegetables immediately, place them in a bowl of water with a little lemon juice to prevent discoloration.

Onions Peeled onions can be spiralized whole – all you need to do is trim the ends before you start. You can use spiralized onions to replace chopped ones in recipes or turn them into crispy onion spirals.

Parsnips Choose large fat parsnips for best results. Add them to a potato pancake or make parsnip crisps.

Pears Choose firm pears for spiralizing, as pears that are too ripe will add too much moisture to some of the dessert recipes. To prepare the pears for spiralizing, just trim down the pointy ends.

Potatoes and sweet potatoes Prepare potatoes by either scrubbing or peeling and then trim the ends and cut in half crosswise if very large. Sweet potatoes are great for adding color to a dish.

Turnips Peel off the outside skin and cut into large chunks with flat ends to attach to the spiralizer. Use in potato cakes or fritters.

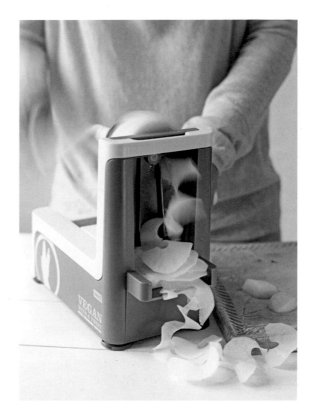

Zucchini Forget about regular pasta, spiralized zucchini make perfect zucchini noodles. They can be eaten raw or very lightly steamed, boiled or stir-fried.

Cooking and storing spiralized vegetables
Spiralized vegetables can be eaten raw or cooked very quickly. The best cooking methods for spiralized vegetables are steaming, stir-frying and simmering in boiling water. You can also bake and roast spiralized vegetables such as potatoes, parsnips, beets and butternut squash in half the time you would cook large chunks of the same vegetables. It is very easy to overcook vegetable "spaghetti", so keep a close eye on it while cooking to make sure it doesn't fall apart.

Most spiralized vegetables can be stored in an airtight container in the refrigerator for up to 4 days, so you can prepare your vegetables in advance or spiralize extra and save the rest for another day. The exceptions are spiralized cucumber, which will only keep for about 2 days because of its high water content, and apples, pears and potatoes, which quickly oxidize and turn brown; they are best prepared as needed.

light bites

vegetable noodle miso soup

Serves 4
Prepare in 5 minutes
Cook in 10 minutes

3 cups (900 ml) hot vegetable stock
2 tablespoons white miso paste
2 teaspoons grated fresh ginger
2 carrots, peeled, ends trimmed and
   halved crosswise
2 zucchini, ends trimmed and halved
   crosswise
5 oz (150 g) fresh or frozen
   shelled edamame
2 tablespoons chopped fresh cilantro

Place the vegetable stock, miso paste and ginger in a saucepan. Bring to a boil, then reduce the heat and simmer for 3–4 minutes.

Meanwhile, using a spiralizer fitted with a 3 mm (⅛ inch) spaghetti blade, spiralize the carrots and zucchini.

Add the spiralized carrots and zucchini and the edamame to the soup and simmer for 3–4 minutes, until just tender. Stir in the cilantro and serve immediately.

light bites

~shrimp rice paper~ wraps

Serves 2
Prepare in 10 minutes

4 inch (10 cm) piece daikon, peeled
    and ends trimmed
½ carrot, peeled and ends trimmed
1 green onion, finely sliced
1 oz (25 g) bean sprouts
4 tablespoons chopped fresh cilantro
125 g (4 oz) cooked peeled shrimp
4 dried rice paper wrappers (banh
    trang), about 8 inches (20.5 cm)
    in diameter (available from Asian
    supermarkets)
1 tablespoon Asian fish sauce
8 mint leaves
Prepared sweet chile sauce,
    for serving

Using a spiralizer fitted with a 3 mm (⅛ inch) spaghetti blade, spiralize the daikon and carrot.

Place the spiralized vegetables in a bowl with the green onion, bean sprouts, cilantro and shrimp and mix well.

One at a time, place each rice paper wrapper in a bowl of warm water for about 30 seconds, until the wrapper softens and turns opaque, and then remove, shake off any excess water and place on a work surface. Brush the middle of the wrapper with a little fish sauce, add 2 mint leaves and then arrange a little of the shrimp and vegetable mixture along the center. Fold over both ends of the wrapper and then roll up and cover with a damp cloth. Repeat with the remaining wrappers and filling.

Cut each roll in half and serve immediately with the chile sauce for dipping.

~zucchini, feta and~ ~mint fritters~

Serves 4
Prepare in 10 minutes
Cook in 15 minutes

3 zucchini, ends trimmed and cut in
   half crosswise
4 green onions, chopped
4 tablespoons chopped mint
4 oz (125 g) self-rising flour
1 teaspoon ground cumin
2 eggs, lightly beaten
Salt and freshly ground black pepper
4 oz (125 g) feta cheese, crumbled
1 tablespoon olive oil, for frying
Prepared tomato salsa, for serving

Using a spiralizer fitted with a 3 mm (⅛ inch) spaghetti blade, spiralize the zucchini.

In a large bowl, mix together the spiralized zucchini, green onions, mint, flour and cumin. Stir in the eggs, mix well and season with salt and pepper. Gently fold in the feta.

Heat the oil in a large frying pan over medium heat. Cooking 4 fritters at a time, add heaped tablespoons of the batter to the pan, flatten slightly and cook for 3 minutes on each side, until golden. Repeat until all the batter is used up. Serve the fritters with the tomato salsa.

Mexican baked potato nests

Serves 4
Prepare in 10 minutes
Cook in 20 minutes

2 russet potatoes, about 12 oz
  (375 g), peeled and ends trimmed
1 small onion, ends trimmed
2 tablespoons olive oil
Salt and freshly ground black pepper
3 oz (75 g) cured Spanish-style
  chorizo, diced
1 garlic clove, crushed
1 mild green chile, seeded and finely
  chopped
½ small yellow bell pepper, cored,
  seeded and diced
One 7 oz (200 g) can chopped
  tomatoes
1 teaspoon tomato ketchup
1 tablespoon chopped fresh cilantro
4 eggs
Smoked paprika, for sprinkling
Salt and freshly ground black pepper

British cooks would use a pan called a Yorkshire pudding tin for this recipe, but you can use a muffin top pan. Each well should be about 4 inches (10 cm) in diameter.

Preheat the oven to 350°F (180°C).

Using a spiralizer fitted with a 3 mm (⅛ inch) spaghetti blade, spiralize the potatoes and onion, keeping them separate.

Place the spiralized potatoes in a large bowl, add the oil, season with salt and pepper and then use your hands to toss the potatoes to coat them in the oil and seasoning. Divide the potatoes between 4 wells of a muffin pan. Bake the potato nests for 10 minutes.

Meanwhile, place the chorizo in a frying pan and cook over medium heat for 2–3 minutes, until the oil has been released from the chorizo. Stir in the spiralized onion, garlic, chile and yellow pepper and cook over medium-high heat, stirring frequently, for about 2–3 minutes, until the pepper is soft. Stir in the tomatoes and ketchup and season with salt and pepper. Bring to a boil, then reduce the heat and simmer for 2–3 minutes, until the mixture has thickened. Stir in the cilantro and season to taste.

Remove the potato nests from the oven and use the back of a spoon to press down the center of each nest to make a hollow. Divide the tomato mixture between the nests and then use the back of a spoon to make 4 shallow wells.

Break an egg into each shallow well (don't worry if the egg runs out slightly). Return to the oven and bake for 6–7 minutes more, until the eggs are just set. Sprinkle a little smoked paprika over the top and serve immediately.

daikon, carrot and cucumber laksa

Serves 4
Prepare in 5 minutes
Cook in 10 minutes

1 lb (500 g) daikon, peeled, ends
   trimmed and halved crosswise
1 large carrot, peeled, ends trimmed
   and halved crosswise
¼ cucumber, ends trimmed
6 tablespoons prepared laksa paste
5 oz (150 g) green beans, trimmed
   and halved
One 13 fl oz (400 ml) can
   coconut milk
2½ cups (750 ml) hot vegetable stock
1 tablespoon palm sugar or light
   brown sugar
4 oz (125 g) bean sprouts
One 7½ oz (225 g) can bamboo
   shoots, drained
2 tablespoons chopped fresh cilantro
4 green onions, chopped
1 red chile, finely sliced
4 lime wedges, for serving

Flat rice noodles are replaced with spiralized daikon in this spicy soup recipe. You could add some cooked shrimp to the dish if you like, stirring them in at the end of the cooking time to heat through. Laksa is a type of soup or curried dish from Indonesia. Look for prepared laksa base, or paste, in Asian food stores or from an online source.

Using a spiralizer fitted with a 6 mm (¼ inch) flat noodle blade, spiralize the daikon. Change to a 3 mm (⅛ inch) spaghetti blade and spiralize the carrot and cucumber, keeping the daikon, carrot and cucumber separate.

Place the laksa paste, spiralized daikon and beans in a large saucepan and stir to coat the vegetables with the paste. Cook over medium heat for 1–2 minutes, then stir in the coconut milk, stock and sugar and simmer for 2 minutes. Add the spiralized carrot, bean sprouts and bamboo shoots and simmer for 3 minutes, until all the vegetables are just tender. Stir in the cilantro.

Divide the soup between 4 bowls and top with the green onions, chile and spiralized cucumber. Serve immediately, with lime wedges to squeeze over.

zucchini and haloumi bruschetta

Serves 2
Prepare in 5 minutes
Cook in 5–10 minutes

1 large zucchini, ends trimmed and
   halved crosswise
1 tablespoon olive oil
1 teaspoon thyme leaves
1 garlic clove, crushed
Salt and freshly ground black pepper
4 slices haloumi cheese
4 slices ciabatta, toasted

Using a spiralizer fitted with a ribbon blade, spiralize the zucchini.
Snip any extra-long ribbons in half with scissors.

In a large bowl, mix together the olive oil, thyme and garlic and
then season with salt and pepper. Gently stir in the spiralized
zucchini to coat it with the oil.

Heat a large griddle over high heat. Add the zucchini in a single
layer and cook for 1–2 minutes, until lightly charred – you may need
to do this in 2 batches. Transfer the zucchini to a plate and set aside.

Add the haloumi to the griddle and cook for 1–2 minutes on
each side, until golden-brown stripes appear and the cheese
starts to melt.

Arrange the toasted ciabatta on 2 plates and place the seared
haloumi and zucchini on top. Serve immediately.

baked apple and cinnamon chips

Serves 4–6
Prepare in 5 minutes, plus cooling
Bake in 1¾–2 hours

2 Granny Smith apples, ends trimmed
1 teaspoon ground cinnamon

I like to use tart cooking apples for this recipe but you can also use any large red or green eating apples. The spiralized apples are slowly baked on a low heat to dry them out, which results in a really crisp and tasty snack.

Preheat the oven to 275°F (140°C).

Line 2 large baking sheets with parchment paper. Using a spiralizer fitted with a ribbon blade, spiralize the apples.

Spread out the spiralized apples in a single layer on the prepared baking sheets and sprinkle with the cinnamon.

Bake for 1 hour. Turn the chips and return to the oven for 45 minutes–1 hour, until the chips are lightly golden. Turn off the oven and leave the chips in the oven to cool and crisp up. The chips will keep for up to 2 days in an airtight container.

Greek salad pita pockets

Serves 4
Prepare in 10 minutes

1 small red onion, ends trimmed
5 inch (12 cm) piece cucumber, ends
  trimmed and cut in half crosswise
8 cherry tomatoes, quartered
6 pitted black olives, chopped
4 oz (125 g) feta cheese, crumbled
1 tablepoon lemon juice
2 tablespoons extra-virgin olive oil
1 teaspoon dried oregano
Salt and freshly ground black pepper
4 pita breads
1 head Little Gem lettuce, shredded

Preheat the broiler.

Using a spiralizer fitted with a 3 mm (⅛ inch) spaghetti blade, spiralize the onion and cucumber.

Place the spiralized onion and cucumber in a large bowl with the tomatoes, olives and feta.

In a small bowl, whisk together the lemon juice, oil and oregano and then season to taste with salt and pepper. Pour the dressing over the salad ingredients and gently toss together.

Toast the pita under the broiler or about 1 minute on each side.

Slice each pita bread in half horizontally. Fill the pita pockets with a little lettuce and then top with the feta mixture. Serve immediately.

mini sweet potato and ricotta frittatas

Makes 8
Prepare in 5 minutes
Bake in 25 minutes

1 tablespoon olive oil, plus a little
    extra for oiling
1 large sweet potato, about 8 oz
    (250 g), peeled, ends trimmed and
    halved crosswise
1 small yellow onion, ends trimmed
2 oz (50 g) baby spinach
6 eggs
2 tablespoons chopped sage
1 tablespoon chopped chives
1 teaspoon paprika
Salt and freshly ground black pepper
4 oz (125 g) ricotta cheese

*These mini frittatas are fantastic for brunch or a light dinner.
To round out the meal, serve them with a crisp green salad.*

Preheat the oven to 350°F (180°C).

Lightly oil 8 wells of a nonstick muffin pan. Using a spiralizer fitted with a 3 mm (⅛ inch) spaghetti blade, spiralize the sweet potato and onion.

Heat the 1 tablespoon oil in a large frying pan over medium heat, add the spiralized sweet potato and onion and cook for 3 minutes, until the sweet potato has softened slightly. Add the spinach and cook for 1 minute, until the spinach has wilted. Allow the mixture to cool slightly.

Beat the eggs in a large bowl with the herbs and paprika and then season with salt and pepper. Add the sweet potato mixture and mix well. Stir in spoonfuls of the ricotta.

Divide the mixture between the wells in the prepared muffin tin and bake for 20 minutes or until set. Serve the frittatas immediately.

salt and vinegar baked potato chips

Serves 4
Prepare in 5 minutes, plus standing
Bake in 45 minutes

2 russet potatoes, skins scrubbed and
   ends trimmed
6 tablespoons malt vinegar
2 teaspoons flaky sea salt,
   for sprinkling

Preheat the oven to 275°F (140°C).

Line 2 large baking sheets with parchment paper. Using
a spiralizer fitted with a ribbon blade, spiralize the potatoes.

Place the spiralized potatoes in a large bowl and add the
vinegar. Toss well to coat in the vinegar and then let stand
for 30 minutes to allow the potatoes to absorb the flavor.

Drain the potatoes and then lay them out in a single layer on
the prepared baking sheets and sprinkle with the salt.

Bake for 30 minutes. Turn the potatoes, removing any chips that
are brown, and return to the oven for 15 minutes more, until the
chips are lightly golden.

Turn off the oven. Return any chips you removed to the baking
sheets and leave the chips in the oven to cool and crisp up. The
chips will keep for up to 2 days in an airtight container.

crab and vegetable dim sum

Serves 4 as a starter
Prepare in 20 minutes
Cook in 10 minutes

1 carrot, peeled and ends trimmed

1 zucchini, ends trimmed

4 oz (125 g) fresh or canned crab meat, picked over

1 inch (2.5 cm) piece fresh ginger, peeled and grated

½ red chile, seeded and finely chopped

1 teaspoon toasted sesame oil

2 teaspoons rice wine vinegar

2 teaspoons dark soy sauce

2 teaspoons cornstarch

16 round Asian dumpling wrappers (available from Asian supermarkets)

For serving
Soy sauce
Prepared sweet chile sauce

Using a spiralizer fitted with a 3 mm (⅛ inch) spaghetti blade, spiralize the carrot and zucchini. Roughly snip any really long spirals in half with scissors.

Place the spiralized vegetables in a large bowl with the crabmeat, ginger, chile, sesame oil, vinegar, soy sauce, and cornstarch. Mix well until thoroughly mixed.

Place a dumpling wrapper on a clean work surface, brush the edges of the wrapper with a little cold water and place a tablespoon of the crab and vegetable mixture in the center. Spread out the mixture along the middle and then fold the wrapper over the filling to make a semi-circle. Crimp the edges together with damp hands. Repeat until all the wrappers and the crab and vegetable mixture have been used.

Place half of the dim sum in a bamboo or metal steamer over a pan of simmering water and cover with a lid. Steam for 4–5 minutes, until the wrappers are translucent and the filling is cooked through. Transfer the dim sum to a warm plate and cover with aluminum foil. Repeat with the remaining dim sum.

Divide the dim sum among 4 plates or arrange on a serving platter and serve immediately with the soy and sweet chile sauce in dipping bowls alongside.

crispy onion bhajis

Makes about 12
Prepare in 10 minutes
Cook in 10 minutes

2 yellow onions, ends trimmed
3½ oz (100 g) chickpea flour
½ teaspoon baking powder
1 green chile, finely chopped
2 tablespoons chopped fresh cilantro
1 teaspoon salt
1 teaspoon ground cumin
½ teaspoon ground turmeric
1 tablespoon sunflower oil
1 teaspoon lemon juice
5–6 tablespoons water
3½ cups (1 litre) vegetable or
   sunflower oil, for deep frying
Cucumber and Mint Raita (see page
   92), for serving

Spiralizing onions is really quick and easy, which means that you can make this delicious Indian-style fritters as a snack or starter in no time at all.

Using a spiralizer fitted with a 6 mm (¼ inch) flat noodle blade, spiralize the onions.

Place the flour, baking powder, chile, cilantro, salt, cumin and turmeric in a large bowl and mix well. Stir in the sunflower oil, lemon juice and enough water to make a thick batter. Add the spiralized onions and stir to coat with the batter.

Heat the vegetable or sunflower oil in a wok or deep, heavy-based saucepan until it reads 350–375°F (180–190°C) on a deep-frying thermometer, or until a cube of bread dropped into the oil turns golden brown in 30 seconds.

Carefully drop tablespoonfuls of the batter into the hot oil, cooking 4 bhajis at a time, and deep-fry for 2–3 minutes, until golden. Remove from the oil with a slotted spoon, drain on paper towels and keep warm while you cook the remaining bhaji mixture. Serve the bhajis hot with the cucumber and mint raita.

spiral vegetable tempura

Serves 4
Prepare in 10 minutes
Cook in 10–20 minutes

10 oz (300 g) mixed vegetables, such
as zucchini, sweet potatoes and
carrots, ends trimmed and cut in
half crosswise
2 cups (600 ml) vegetable oil,
for frying

For the batter
7 oz (200 g) all-purpose flour
1 tablespoon cornstarch
1 cup (300 ml) cold sparkling water
2 ice cubes

Flaky sea salt, for sprinkling

*For perfect tempura, make the batter just before cooking
and ensure that the oil is the correct temperature so that
the batter remains light and crispy.*

Using a spiralizer fitted with a ribbon blade, spiralize the vegetables.

Preheat the oven to 300°F (150°C).

Heat the oil in a wok or deep, heavy-based saucepan until it
reads 350–375°F (180–190°C) on a deep-frying thermometer,
or until a cube of bread dropped into the oil turns golden brown
in 30 seconds.

While the oil is heating, make the batter. Place the flour and
cornstarch in a large bowl and slowly whisk in the sparkling water
to make a batter about the consistency of double cream. Add the
ice cubes to the batter and whisk again.

Working in batches, dip a few of the vegetable spirals into the
batter, shake off any excess and carefully drop the battered
vegetables into the hot oil. Deep-fry for 3–4 minutes, until lightly
golden and crisp. Remove the vegetables from the oil with a slotted
spoon, drain on paper towels and then place on a baking sheet
and keep warm in the oven. Repeat until you have used up all the
vegetables and batter. Sprinkle with salt and serve immediately.

fall vegetable minestrone

Serves 4
Prepare in 15 minutes
Cook in 15 minutes

1 yellow onion, ends trimmed
½ small celery root, peeled and
    cut into chunks
2 carrots, peeled, ends trimmed
    and halved crosswise
1 zucchini, ends trimmed and
    halved crosswise
1 tablespoon olive oil
1 garlic clove, crushed
3 oz (75 g) pancetta, cubed
One 13 oz (400 g) can chopped
    tomatoes
2½ cups (750 ml) hot vegetable stock
⅓ head Savoy cabbage, thinly sliced
One 13 oz (400 g) can borlotti or
    kidney beans, drained and rinsed
Salt and freshly ground black pepper

For serving
Freshly grated Parmesan cheese
Basil leaves
Crusty bread

Using a spiralizer fitted with a 3 mm (⅛ inch) spaghetti blade, spiralize the onion, celery root, carrots and zucchini, keeping them separate.

Heat the oil in a large saucepan. Add the spiralized onion and celery root and the garlic and pancetta and cook over low heat for 3–4 minutes, until the onion is soft but not browned. Add the spiralized carrots, tomatoes, stock, cabbage and beans, cover and simmer for 5 minutes, or until the celery root is just tender. Stir in the spiralized zucchini, cover and cook for 3–4 minutes more, or until all the vegetables are tender. Season the soup to taste.

Ladle the soup into 4 bowls, sprinkle with the Parmesan and basil leaves and serve with chunks of crusty bread.

light bites

27

smoked haddock chowder

Serves 4
Prepare in 5 minutes
Cook in 15 minutes

1 yellow onion, ends trimmed
8 oz (225 g) russet potatoes, peeled
   and ends trimmed
1 oz (25 g) unsalted butter
4 slices lean smoked bacon, chopped
1½ cups (450 ml) milk
1 cup (300 ml) fish stock or clam juice
Freshly ground black pepper
5 oz (150 g) frozen corn kernels
1 lb (500 g) undyed smoked haddock
   fillets, skinned and cut into chunks
3½ oz (100 g) baby spinach
crusty bread, for serving

This creamy chowder is a warming and hearty soup that's packed full of haddock, spiralized potatoes, sweet corn and wilted baby spinach.

Using a spiralizer fitted with a 3 mm (⅛ inch) spaghetti blade, spiralize the onion. Change to a 6 mm (¼ inch) flat noodle blade and spiralize the potatoes, keeping the onion and potatoes separate.

Melt the butter in a large saucepan over a medium heat. Add the spiralized onion and cook for 2 minutes. Add the bacon and cook for 3 minutes, until browned. Pour in the milk and stock, stir in the spiralized potatoes and then bring to a boil. Season well with pepper, reduce the heat, cover and simmer over low heat for 3–4 minutes, or until the potatoes are just tender. Stir in the corn and haddock and gently simmer for 3–4 minutes, until the fish starts to flake. Stir in the spinach.

As soon as the spinach has wilted, ladle the soup into bowls. Serve with crusty bread.

pumpkin, cheese and chive muffins

Makes 10
Prepare in 10 minutes
Bake in 20–25 minutes

Large chunk of cheese pumpkin or
    butternut squash (the non-bulbous
    end), about 9 oz (275 g), peeled
9 oz (275 g) all-purpose flour
1 tablespoon baking powder
4 oz (125 g) aged Cheddar cheese,
    shredded
2 tablespoons chopped chives
2 eggs
6 fl oz (175 ml) milk
3 oz (75 g) butter, melted
2 tablespoons shelled pumpkin seeds

Preheat the oven to 375°F (190°C).

Line a muffin pan with 10 paper muffin liners. Using a spiralizer fitted with a 3 mm (⅛ inch) spaghetti blade, spiralize the pumpkin or squash. Roughly snip any long strands in half with scissors.

In a large bowl, sift together the flour and baking powder. Stir in the cheese and chives and mix well.

In a separate bowl, beat together the eggs, milk and melted butter.

Pour the wet ingredients over the dry ingredients and stir until just combined. Stir in the spiralized pumpkin or squash.

Divide the mixture among the muffin cups and then sprinkle the tops with the pumpkin seeds. Bake for 20–25 minutes, until risen and firm. Serve warm or at room temperature.

baked vegetable chips

Serves 4
Prepare in 10 minutes
Bake in 30–35 minutes

1 sweet potato, peeled, ends trimmed
   and halved crosswise
1 large parsnip, peeled, ends trimmed
   and halved crosswise
2 fresh beets, scrubbed and ends
   trimmed
2 tablespoons olive oil
Flaky sea salt

These colorful oven-baked vegetable chips make a healthy alternative to deep-fried potato chips. Any leftovers can be stored for 1–2 days in an airtight container.

Preheat the oven to 325°F (160°C).

Line 2 large baking sheets with parchment paper. Using a spiralizer fitted with a ribbon blade, spiralize the sweet potato, parsnip and beet.

Place the spiralized vegetables in a large bowl, drizzle with the oil, sprinkle with a little sea salt and mix well.

Spread out the vegetables in a single layer on the prepared baking sheets. Bake for 15 minutes. Turn the vegetables, removing any chips that are brown, and return to the oven for 15–20 minutes more, until the chips are lightly golden.

Turn off the oven. Return any chips you removed to the baking sheets and leave the chips in the oven to cool and crisp up – the chips will become extra crispy as they cool. Sprinkle with a little extra sea salt and serve.

salads

chicken, zucchini and quinoa salad

Serves 4
Prepare in 10 minutes
Cook in 20–30 minutes

7 oz (200 g) quinoa, rinsed
Salt and freshly ground black pepper
2 zucchini, ends trimmed and halved
   crosswise
1 tablespoon olive oil
2 teaspoons sumac
3 boneless, skinless chicken breast
   halves
Finely grated zest and juice of
   1 large organic lemon
1 tablespoon extra-virgin olive oil
4 tablespoons chopped fresh mint
3½ oz (100 g) pistachios, roughly
   chopped
5 oz (150 g) pomegranate seeds

Searing the zucchini ribbons gives them a lovely smoky flavor. Be careful not to overcook the zucchini or they will become mushy.

Place the quinoa in a saucepan, cover with 2 cups (600 ml) cold water and add a little salt. Bring to a boil, then reduce the heat and simmer for 10–15 minutes or until the quinoa is tender and has absorbed most of the water. Remove from the heat, cover and let stand while you prepare the rest of the salad.

Using a spiralizer fitted with a ribbon blade, spiralize the zucchini.

Place the olive oil and sumac in shallow dish and season with salt and pepper. Add the chicken and toss to coat.

Heat a griddle over medium heat until hot. Add the chicken and cook for 4– 6 minutes on each side or until cooked through. Transfer the chicken to a plate and set aside.

Add the spiralized zucchini to the griddle and cook for about 2 minutes or until lightly browned.

Place the quinoa in a large bowl, add the lemon zest and juice, extra-virgin olive oil, mint and pistachios, mix well and season to taste. Gently stir in the zucchini and pomegranate seeds.

Thinly slice the chicken breasts. Divide the quinoa salad between 4 plates, top with the chicken and serve immediately.

Japanese tuna tataki salad

**Serves 2 as a main course
or 4 as a starter**
Prepare in 20 minutes
Cook in 2 minutes

8 oz (250 g) daikon, peeled, ends
    trimmed and halved crosswise
½ cucumber, ends trimmed and
    halved crosswise

For the dressing
2 tablespoons Japanese soy sauce
Finely grated zest and juice of
    1 organic lime
1 teaspoon grated fresh ginger
2 teaspoons yuzu juice (or use
    grapefruit juice)
2 tablespoons mirin
1 tablespoon honey

2 tablespoons sesame seeds
1 tablespoon black peppercorns
Pinch of salt
Two 6 oz (175 g) tuna steaks, about
    1 inch (2.5 cm) thick
1 tablespoon sunflower oil
Wasabi paste, for serving

Using a spiralizer fitted with a 3 mm (⅛ inch) spaghetti blade, spiralize the daikon and cucumber. Place the spiralized vegetables in a bowl of ice-cold water and place in the refrigerator.

Now make the dressing. Whisk together the soy sauce, lime zest and juice, ginger, yuzu juice, mirin and honey in a small bowl. Set aside.

Toast the sesame seeds in a dry frying pan over a medium heat for 2 minutes, until just golden. Allow to cool.

Roughly crush the peppercorns in a pestle with a mortar, then add the toasted sesame seeds and a pinch of salt and grind until everything is roughly crushed.

Pour the sesame mixture onto a plate and spread out. Gently press the tuna steaks into the sesame mixture, turning over and repeating until evenly coated.

Heat the oil in a large nonstick frying pan over medium heat. Add the tuna steaks and cook for 1 minute on each side, until the outside is cooked but the middle is still pink. Remove from the pan and set aside to rest.

Drain the cucumber and daikon and pat dry with paper towels. Divide the vegetables among 4 plates or place on a large platter.

Thinly slice the tuna and arrange on top of the cucumber and daikon. Drizzle with some of the dressing and serve immediately with the remaining dressing and wasabi paste alongside.

butternut squash, feta and Puy lentil salad

Serves 4
Prepare in 10 minutes
Cook in 20 minutes

½ butternut squash (the non-
  bulbous end), about 1 lb (500 g),
  peeled and halved crosswise
3 tablespoons olive oil
1 teaspoon cumin seeds
Salt and freshly ground black pepper
Juice of 1 small lemon
1 teaspoon Dijon mustard
8 oz (250 g) cooked Puy lentils
1 oz (25 g) walnut pieces
4 oz (125 g) feta cheese, crumbled
3½ oz (100 g) baby spinach

Preheat the oven to 375°F (190°C).

Using a spiralizer fitted with a 3 mm (⅛ inch) spaghetti blade, spiralize the squash.

Place the spiralized squash in a large bowl, add 1 tablespoon of the oil and the cumin seeds and season with salt and pepper. Mix well to coat the squash with the oil, cumin seeds and seasoning.

Spread out the squash on a large nonstick baking sheet and roast for about 20 minutes, stirring halfway through, until golden and starting to crisp. Remove from the oven and let cool slightly.

In a small bowl, whisk together the remaining 2 tablespoons oil with the lemon juice and mustard and season to taste with salt and pepper.

Place the squash, lentils, walnuts, feta and spinach in a large bowl, pour over the lemon and mustard mixture and gently toss together. Serve immediately in bowls.

Thai beef salad

Serves 4
Prepare in 15 minutes
Cook in 10–15 minutes

For the dressing
2 tablespoons palm sugar or light
    brown sugar
2 tablespoons Asian fish sauce
Juice of 3 limes
3 garlic cloves, crushed
1 bird's eye chile, seeded and finely
    chopped
6 tablespoons chopped fresh cilantro

1 small cucumber, ends trimmed and
    halved crosswise
2 carrots, peeled, ends trimmed and
    halved crosswise
1 small daikon, peeled, ends trimmed
    and halved crosswise
1 lb (500 g) sirloin steak
1 tablespoon sunflower or peanut oil
Salt and freshly ground black pepper
½ head Napa cabbage or iceberg
    lettuce, finely sliced
Handful of peanuts, roughly chopped
    (optional)

First, make the dressing. Whisk together the sugar, fish sauce, lime juice, garlic, chile and cilantro in a small bowl until the sugar has dissolved.

Using a spiralizer fitted with a 3 mm (⅛ inch) spaghetti blade, spiralize the cucumber, carrots and daikon.

Place the spiralized vegetables in a bowl and drizzle with half the dressing. Let the salad marinate while you cook the steak.

Brush the steak with the oil and season with salt and pepper. Heat a griddle over high heat until smoking hot, then add the steak and cook over medium-high heat for 3–6 minutes on each side, or until cooked to your liking. Transfer the steak to a plate and allow to rest for 5 minutes, then thinly slice.

Just before you are ready to serve, stir the cabbage or lettuce into the bowl with the spiralized vegetables. Divide the salad among 4 plates or place on a large platter, top with the steak and drizzle with the remaining dressing. Sprinkle with the peanuts, if using, and serve immediately.

Jerusalem artichoke and bacon salad

Serves 4
Prepare in 12 minutes
Cook in 10 minutes

2 tablespoons olive oil
8 slices lean smoked bacon, chopped
1 garlic clove, crushed
12 oz (350 g) large Jerusalem
   artichokes, scrubbed
2 tablespoons flat-leaf parsley
2 tablespoons balsamic vinegar
1 tablespoon lemon juice
Salt and freshly ground black pepper
8 heads Little Gem lettuce, quartered
Small handful of Parmesan cheese
   shavings

Jerusalem artichokes are sometimes labled "sunchokes" at the market. They have a delicious, nutty flavor.

Heat 1 tablespoon of the oil in a large frying pan or wok over medium heat. Add the bacon and garlic and cook for 2–3 minutes, stirring occasionally, until the bacon is lightly browned.

Meanwhile, using a spiralizer fitted with a ribbon blade, spiralize the Jerusalem artichokes. Snip any extra-long ribbons in half with scissors.

Immediately add the spiralized Jerusalem artichokes to the bacon in the frying pan (to prevent discoloring) and stir-fry for 3–4 minutes, until the bacon and Jerusalem artichokes start to turn crispy. Remove from the heat and stir in the parsley.

In a small bowl, whisk together the remaining 1 tablespoon oil, the vinegar and lemon juice and season to taste with salt and pepper.

Divide the lettuce among 4 plates and top with the warm bacon and Jerusalem artichoke mixture. Spoon over a little of the dressing, sprinkle with Parmesan shavings and serve immediately.

smoked salmon salad ~with dill and lemon~

Serves 4

Prepare in 10 minutes, plus marinating

1 large fennel bulb, ends trimmed

1 zucchini, ends trimmed and halved crosswise

½ cucumber, ends trimmed and halved crosswise

2 teaspoons finely chopped dill

2 tablespoons lemon juice

1 tablespoon olive oil

1 teaspoon superfine sugar

½ teaspoon flaky sea salt

8 slices smoked salmon

Lemon wedges, for serving

This tasty salad combines spiralized crunchy vegetables in a dill and lemony dressing with delicious smoked salmon. It can be served either as a main course or starter.

Using a spiralizer fitted with a ribbon blade, spiralize the fennel, zucchini and cucumber. Pat the cucumber dry on paper towels.

Place the spiralized vegetables in a large bowl and add the dill, lemon juice, oil, sugar and salt. Toss well to combine and let marinate for 10 minutes.

Divide the vegetables among 4 plates or arrange on a platter, top with the salmon and serve immediately with lemon wedges to squeeze over.

smoked mackerel and quail egg salad

Serves 4
Prepare in 10 minutes
Cook in 20 minutes

For the crispy potato straws
2 russet potatoes, peeled and ends
  trimmed
1 tablespoon olive oil
Salt and freshly ground black pepper

12 quail eggs

For the dressing
2 tablespoons olive oil
2 teaspoons grainy mustard
1 tablespoon white wine vinegar
1 teaspoon honey
1 tablespoon chopped chives

6 oz (175 g) watercress or arugula
  leaves
12 oz (375 g) smoked peppered
  mackerel fillets, skin removed and
  broken into large flakes
16 cherry tomatoes, halved

The potato straws provide a lovely crisp contrast in this salad. You can replace the quail eggs with 4 chicken eggs, if you prefer, increasing the cooking time for the eggs to 6–8 minutes.

Preheat the oven to 350°F (180°C).

First, make the crispy potato straws. Using a spiralizer fitted with a 3 mm (⅛ inch) spaghetti blade, spiralize the potatoes. Place the spiralized potatoes in a large bowl, add the oil, season with salt and pepper and toss together to coat. Line a large baking sheet with parchment paper and arrange the potatoes on the baking sheet in a single layer. Bake for 10 minutes, then turn the potatoes, removing any potatoes that are already browned, and bake for 10 minutes more or until golden and crispy. Allow to cool.

Meanwhile, cook the quail eggs in a saucepan of boiling water for 3 minutes. Drain the eggs, refresh in cold water, then shell and halve them.

To make the dressing, whisk together the oil, mustard, vinegar and honey in a small bowl. Season to taste and stir in the chives.

Toss the watercress or arugula leaves with a little of the dressing and divide among 4 plates. Top with the smoked mackerel, quail eggs and tomatoes, drizzle with the remaining dressing and top with the crispy potato straws. Serve immediately.

apple, endive and walnut salad

Serves 2
Prepare in 10 minutes

For the dressing
Juice of ½ lemon
1 tablespoon walnut or light olive oil
1 teaspoon Dijon mustard
1 teaspoon honey
Salt and freshly ground black pepper

1 large red apple, ends trimmed
1 head white Belgian endive,
  leaves separated
1 head red Belgian endive,
  leaves separated
2 oz (50 g) watercress
1 oz (25 g) walnuts, chopped

The sweetness of the apple perfectly balances the bitterness of the endive in this simple salad. Serve it on its own or as an accompaniment for grilled meat.

First make the dressing. In a small bowl, whisk together the lemon juice, oil, mustard and honey and then season to taste with a little salt and pepper.

Using a spiralizer fitted with a ribbon blade, spiralize the apple.

Arrange the spiralized apple, endive and watercress on a large platter. Drizzle with the dressing and gently toss together. Sprinkle with the walnuts and serve immediately.

green papaya and chicken salad

Serves 4
Prepare in 15 minutes,
  plus marinating

1 large green papaya, peeled
  and ends trimmed

For the dressing
Juice of 2 limes
1 teaspoon palm sugar or
  light brown sugar
1 red chile, seeded and
  finely chopped
2 teaspoons finely grated
  fresh ginger
2 teaspoons dark soy sauce

4 green onions, finely sliced
8 oz (250 g) cooked skinless chicken
  breasts, shredded
4 tablespoons chopped cilantro
Small handful fresh mint leaves,
  for garnish
Lime wedges, for serving

Green, or unripe, papayas are long green fruit that are available in supermarkets and Asian grocery stores. The strips of papaya and shredded chicken in this light and fragrant Thai-style salad soak up the delicious chile and lime dressing beautifully.

Cut the papaya in half crosswise and tap out the seeds. Attach the narrow end of one half of the papaya to a spiralizer fitted with a 3 mm (⅛ inch) spaghetti blade and spiralize the papaya. Repeat with the remaining papaya half.

To make the dressing, place the lime juice, sugar, chile, ginger and soy sauce in a small bowl and whisk until the sugar has dissolved.

Place the spiralized papaya in a large bowl, add the green onions and shredded chicken and pour over the dressing. Toss well and let marinate for about 10 minutes.

Stir the cilantro into the salad. Garnish the salad with mint leaves and serve with lime wedges to squeeze over.

Vietnamese chicken and noodle salad

Serves 4
Prepare in 10 minutes

5 oz (150 g) instant rice vermicelli
2 carrots, peeled, ends trimmed and
   halved crosswise
½ cucumber, ends trimmed
8 oz (250 g) cooked skinless chicken
   breasts, shredded
3 oz (75 g) bean sprouts
4 tablespoons chopped mint
4 tablespoons chopped cilantro
2 oz (50 g) roasted peanuts, chopped

For the dressing
2 tablespoons rice wine vinegar
3 tablespoons prepared sweet chile
   sauce
1 tablespoon Asian fish sauce
4 tablespoons lime juice

For garnishing
Cilantro leaves
Mint leaves

Place the noodles in a large bowl and pour in boiling water to cover. Let stand for 3 minutes, then refresh under cold water and drain.

Meanwhile, using a spiralizer fitted with a 6 mm (¼ inch) flat noodle blade, spiralize the carrots and cucumber.

Place the spiralized vegetables in a large bowl with the chicken, bean sprouts, chopped herbs, peanuts and noodles.

In a small bowl, whisk together the vinegar, chile sauce, fish sauce and lime juice.

Pour the dressing over the noodle salad and toss well. Divide the salad among 4 bowls, garnish with cilantro and mint leaves and serve immediately.

pear, ham and blue cheese salad

Serves 2
Prepare in 5 minutes

1 large or 2 small red-skinned pears, pointy ends trimmed
Juice of 1 lemon
1 tablespoon extra-virgin olive oil
Salt and freshly ground black pepper
3½ oz (100 g) arugula leaves
4 thin slices Serrano ham or prosciutto
3 oz (75 g) Roquefort or Gorgonzola cheese, cubed

The red-skinned pears are very pretty but you can use green-skinned pears if you prefer. The crunchy texture of the pears works really well with the creamy blue cheese.

Using a spiralizer fitted with a 6 mm (¼ inch) flat noodle blade, spiralize the pears. Place the spiralized pears in a bowl and toss with a little of the lemon juice, to prevent them from turning brown.

To make a dressing, whisk together the remaining lemon juice and the oil in a small bowl and season with salt and pepper.

Divide the arugula leaves between 2 plates, top with the pear and slices of ham and scatter the cheese over the top. Drizzle with the dressing and serve immediately.

beet, smoked trout and horseradish salad

Serves 2
Prepare in 10 minutes

2 beets, scrubbed and ends trimmed
2 tablespoons crème fraîche
2 tablespoons plain Greek yogurt
1 tablespoon prepared creamed
   horseradish
2 teaspoons white wine vinegar
3½ oz (100 g) watercress
8 oz (250 g) hot-smoked trout fillets,
   broken into large flakes
Freshly ground black pepper

Raw beets contain lots of vitamin C and iron, which will give your immune system a boost.

Using a spiralizer fitted with a 3 mm (⅛ inch) spaghetti blade, spiralize the beets.

In a large bowl, mix together the crème fraîche, yogurt, horseradish sauce and vinegar. Add the spiralized beets and gently stir until evenly coated.

Divide the watercress between 2 plates, top with the beets and arrange the trout over the top. Sprinkle with some pepper and serve immediately.

mains

butternut squash, sage and goat cheese tart

Serves 6–8
Prepare in 10 minutes
Bake in 1 hour

Prepared pie dough for a 10-inch
(25-cm) pie
½ butternut squash (the non-bulbous
end), about 1 lb (500 g), peeled
and halved crosswise
1 tablespoon olive oil
4 slices lean smoked bacon
1 garlic clove, crushed
5 oz (150 g) goat cheese, roughly
chopped
1 cup (300 ml) heavy cream
3 eggs
Salt and freshly ground black pepper
8 sage leaves

Preheat the oven to 375°F (190°C).

On a lightly floured work surface, roll out the dough until large enough to fit a 10 inch (25 cm) tart pan with removeable bottom. Line the pan with the dough. Prick the base with a fork, cover with parchment paper and fill with pie weights. Place the pan on a baking sheet and bake for 15 minutes. Remove the pie weights and paper and return to the oven for 5 minutes, until golden.

Meanwhile, using a spiralizer fitted with a 3 mm (⅛ inch) spaghetti blade, spiralize the squash. You should end up with about 12 oz (375 g) spiralized squash.

Heat the oil in a large frying pan over medium heat and cook the bacon for 2–3 minutes, until lightly browned. Add the garlic and cook for 1 minute, then add the squash and sauté for 2–3 minutes, until slightly softened. Arrange the squash mixture in the dough-lined pan and scatter with half of the goat cheese.

Beat together the cream and eggs in a bowl and then season with salt and pepper. Pour the egg mixture over the butternut squash. Sprinkle with the remaining goat cheese and the sage leaves.

Bake for 40 minutes, until the top is golden and the filling is set. Let cool for 5 minutes, then cut the tart into slices and serve.

shepherd's pie with crispy topping

Serves 4
Prepare in 10 minutes
Bake in 40–50 minutes

1 yellow onion, ends trimmed
2 carrots, peeled, ends trimmed and
    halved crosswise
1 lb (500 g) minced beef
1 tablespoon all-purpose flour
1 cup (300 ml) hot beef stock
1 tablespoon tomato purée
1 tablespoon Worcestershire sauce
1 tablespoon dried mixed herbs

For the crispy topping
2 parsnips, peeled and ends trimmed
2 large russet potatoes, peeled, ends
    trimmed and halved crosswise
3½ oz (100 g) aged Cheddar cheese,
    shredded

Steamed shredded green cabbage,
    for serving

Using a spiralizer fitted with a 3 mm (⅛ inch) spaghetti blade, spiralize the onion and carrots, keeping them separate.

Place the ground beef and spiralized onion in a large saucepan and dry-fry over medium heat for 3–4 minutes, until the beef is browned. Add the spiralized carrots and stir in the flour, cook for 1 minute and then stir in the stock, tomato purée, Worcestershire sauce and herbs. Bring to a boil, reduce the heat, partially cover and simmer for 15–20 minutes, until the liquid has reduced and thickened.

Preheat the oven to 350°F (180°C).

Meanwhile, make the topping. Using a spiralizer fitted with a 3 mm (⅛ inch) spaghetti blade, spiralize the parsnips and potatoes. Place the spiralized parsnips and potatoes in a saucepan of boiling water and cook for 2–3 minutes, until just tender. Drain well and allow to cool slightly. Transfer the parsnips and potatoes to a large bowl, add the cheese and stir to mix well.

Transfer the beef mixture to a 6-cup baking dish and cover with the topping. Bake for 20–25 minutes, until the topping is crispy and the filling is bubbling. Serve with the steamed shredded green cabbage.

zucchini spaghetti with crab, ~chile and lemon~

Serves 2
Prepare in 5 minutes
Cook in 5 minutes

2 large zucchini, ends trimmed and
    halved crosswise
1 tablespoon olive oil
1 garlic clove, crushed
1 small red chile, seeded and finely
    chopped
100 g (3½ oz) fresh white crabmeat,
    picked over
Finely grated zest and juice of
    ½ organic lemon
1 tablespoon chopped mint
Freshly ground black pepper

Using a spiralizer fitted with a 3 mm (⅛ inch) spaghetti blade, spiralize the zucchini.

Heat the oil in a wok or large frying pan over medium heat, add the garlic and chile and cook gently for 2 minutes. Stir in the spiralized zucchini and cook for 2–3 minutes, until just tender. Stir in the crab, lemon zest and juice and mint, gently toss together and season with pepper. Serve immediately.

baked chicken with sweet potatoes

Serves 4
Prepare in 10 minutes
Bake in 30–35 minutes

Finely grated zest and juice of
   2 organic lemons, reserving
   the squeezed lemon halves
1 tablespoon dried oregano
2 teaspoons dried thyme
2 teaspoons smoked paprika
3½ fl oz (100 ml) white wine or
   chicken stock
2 tablespoons olive oil
Salt and freshly ground black pepper
13 oz (400 g) sweet potatoes, peeled
   and ends trimmed
4 chicken thighs
4 chicken drumsticks
6 garlic cloves, unpeeled
14 pitted green olives
Steamed green beans or broccoli,
   for serving

The spiralized sweet potatoes cook really quickly in this traybake recipe, making it the ideal dish for a speedy midweek supper.

Preheat the oven to 375°F (190°C).

In a large liquid measuring cup, mix together the lemon zest and juice, dried herbs, paprika, white wine or stock and olive oil and season well with salt and pepper. Set aside.

Using a spiralizer fitted with a 3 mm (⅛ inch) spaghetti blade, spiralize the sweet potatoes.

Place the chicken, spiralized sweet potatoes and garlic cloves in a large roasting pan. Pour the lemony mixture over the chicken and potatoes and mix everything together until well coated. Arrange the chicken pieces, skin-side up on the top of the sweet potatoes and tuck in the reserved squeezed lemon halves.

Roast for 20 minutes. Baste the chicken and potatoes with the lemony sauce and add the olives. Return to the oven and cook for 10–15 minutes more or until the chicken is golden brown and the potatoes are tender. Serve with steamed green beans or broccoli.

curried sweet potato puffs

Makes 6
Prepare in 10 minutes
Bake in 25–30 minutes

1 yellow onion, ends trimmed
2 sweet potatoes, about 13 oz
    (400 g), peeled, ends trimmed
    and halved crosswise
1 tablespoon sunflower oil
2 tablespoons Thai red curry paste
4 tablespoons unsweetened coconut
    cream
2 tablespoons chopped cilantro
Salt and freshly ground black pepper
All-purpose flour, for dusting
12 oz (375 g) prepared, all-butter
    puff pastry
1 beaten egg, for brushing

Preheat the oven to 375°F (190°C).

Using a spiralizer fitted with a 3 mm (⅛ inch) spaghetti blade, spiralize the onion and sweet potatoes, keeping them separate.

Heat the oil in a large saucepan or frying pan with a lid over medium heat. Add the spiralized onion and cook for 1–2 minutes, until softened. Stir in the curry paste and cook for 1 minute, then stir in the coconut cream until smooth. Add the spiralized sweet potatoes. Cover and simmer for 2–3 minutes, until the sweet potatoes start to soften. Allow the mixture to cool slightly and then stir in the cilantro and season to taste with salt and pepper.

On a lightly-floured work surface, roll out the pastry until about 5 mm (¼ inch) thick. Cut out six 6-inch (15-cm) rounds. Divide the sweet potato mixture between the pastry circles, piling it in the center of each circle. Brush the edges of the pastry with a little beaten egg and then fold over the pastry to cover the filling and form a semi-circle. Pinch or crimp the edges together between your forefinger and thumb to seal.

Transfer the parcels to a nonstick baking sheet, gently prick the sides of the pastry with a fork and then brush the tops of the parcels with the beaten egg. Bake for 20 minutes, until puffed and golden. These sweet potato puffs are delicious served both hot and at room temperature.

butternut squash with ~sage and pine nuts~

Serves 2
Prepare in 5 minutes
Cook in 10 minutes

½ butternut squash (the non-bulbous
    end), about 1 lb (500 g), peeled
    and halved crosswise
1 oz (25 g) unsalted butter
8 sage leaves
1 oz (25 g) pine nuts
1 oz (25 g) Parmesan cheese,
    shredded
Freshly ground black pepper

Using a spiralizer fitted with a 3 mm (⅛ inch) spaghetti blade, spiralize the squash. You should end up with about 12 oz (375 g) spiralized squash.

Place the butter in a large frying pan over medium heat. When the butter starts to foam, stir in the sage leaves and pine nuts and cook for 1–2 minutes, until the sage is crispy and the pine nuts are lightly golden. Add the squash and sauté for 5–6 minutes or until the squash is tender. Remove from the heat and stir in half of the Parmesan.

Divide the squash between 2 bowls, sprinkle with the remaining Parmesan and season with plenty of pepper.

shrimp pad Thai

Serves 2
Prepare in 15 minutes
Cook in 10 minutes

For the noodle sauce
2 tablespoons tamarind paste
2 tablespoons Asian fish sauce
2 tablespoons palm sugar or light
    brown sugar
Juice of 1 lime

1 daikon, about 12 oz (375 g),
    peeled, ends trimmed and halved
    crosswise
1 carrot, ends trimmed and halved
    crosswise
2 tablespoons peanut or sunflower oil
1 garlic clove, chopped
1 red chile, seeded and finely
    chopped
1 bunch of green onions, sliced
4 oz (125 g) raw shelled shrimp
2 eggs, beaten
7 oz (200 g) bean sprouts
4 lime wedges, for serving
2 tablespoons blanched peanuts,
    toasted and roughly chopped
4 tablespoons chopped cilantro

This recipe for pad Thai replaces traditional flat rice noodles with spiralized daikon, making it an ideal dish for those on a low-carb diet.

First, make the noodle sauce. In a small bowl, whisk together the tamarind paste, fish sauce, sugar and lime juice.

Using a spiralizer fitted with a 6 mm (¼ inch) flat noodle blade, spiralize the daikon. Change to a 3 mm (⅛ inch) spaghetti blade and spiralize the carrot, keeping the mooli and carrot separate.

Heat a wok over a high heat, then add 1 tablespoon of the oil and swirl around. Add the garlic, chile and green onions and stir-fry for 1 minute, stirring continuously. Add the spiralized daikon and stir-fry for 2 minutes, then add the spiralized carrots and shrimp and stir-fry for 1–2 minutes or until the shrimp have turned pink.

Push the stir-fried ingredients to the side of the wok and add the remaining 1 tablespoon oil. Pour in the eggs and cook, stirring continuously, until they begin to set.

Add the bean sprouts and pour over the noodle sauce. Toss everything together until heated through, stirring continuously for 2 minutes. Stir in half of the peanuts and cilantro, then spoon into bowls. Serve immediately topped with the remaining peanuts and cilantro with lime wedges to squeeze over.

Spanish chorizo tortilla

Serves 6
Prepare in 10 minutes
Cook in 20–25 minutes

1 large yellow onion, ends trimmed
14½ oz (450 g) russet potatoes,
    peeled and ends trimmed
2 tablespoons olive oil
6 oz (175 g) cured, Spanish-style
    chorizo, diced
5 eggs
2 tablespoons flat-leaf parsley
Salt and freshly ground black pepper
1 teaspoon smoked paprika, for
    sprinkling

A tortilla made with spiralized potatoes will cook more quickly than a traditional tortilla made with sliced potatoes.

Using a spiralizer fitted with a 3 mm (⅛ inch) spaghetti blade, spiralize the onion and potatoes, keeping them separate.

Heat 1 tablespoon of the olive oil in an 8 inch (20 cm) nonstick frying pan with a lid over medium heat. Add the chorizo and spiralized onion and cook for 2–3 minutes, until the onion has softened and the red oil has been released from the chorizo. Add the spiralized potatoes and stir to coat in the oil and onion mixture. Cover and cook for 5 minutes, turning the potatoes once and shaking the pan from time to time, until the potatoes are just tender.

Preheat the broiler.

In a large bowl, beat together the eggs and parsley and season with salt and pepper. Add the potato mixture and stir thoroughly to combine.

Heat the remaining 1 tablespoon oil in the same frying pan and pour in the egg and potato mixture. Cook over low heat for 8–10 minutes, without stirring, until the eggs are set on the bottom.

Place the frying pan under the broiler and cook for 2–3 minutes, until the top of the tortilla is set and golden brown.

Transfer the tortilla to a cutting board. Sprinkle the tortilla with the smoked paprika, cut into wedges and serve.

sesame and ginger salmon en papilotte

Serves 2
Prepare in 10 minutes
Bake in 12–15 minutes

1 inch (2.5 cm) piece fresh
  ginger, peeled and cut into thin
  matchsticks
2 tablespoons light soy sauce
2 tablespoons rice wine vinegar
1 teaspoon toasted sesame oil
1 carrot, peeled, ends trimmed and
  halved crosswise
1 zucchini, ends trimmed and halved
  crosswise
4 green onions, thinly sliced
2 skinless salmon fillets, about 7 oz
  (200 g) each
2 teaspoons sesame seeds, toasted
Steamed rice, for serving

*The spiralized carrot and zucchini will steam perfectly
in the paper parcel with the salmon and ginger.*

Preheat the oven to 400°F (200°C).

In a small bowl, mix together the ginger, soy sauce, rice wine
vinegar and sesame oil to make a sauce.

Using a spiralizer fitted with a 3 mm (⅛ inch) spaghetti blade,
spiralize the carrot and zucchini.

Place two 9-inch (23-cm) squares of parchment paper on a large
baking sheet. Divide the spiralized vegetables and the green onions
between the 2 sheets of paper and then place a salmon fillet on top
of each pile of vegetables. Drizzle with the sauce and then sprinkle
with the sesame seeds. Fold the paper securely to seal the parcel.

Bake the parcels for 12–15 minutes, until the salmon is opaque and
the fish flakes easily. Transfer the parcels to plates, carefully open up
the parcels and serve with steamed rice.

easy potato moussaka

Serves 4
Prepare in 10 minutes
Bake in 50–55 minutes

1 large yellow onion, ends trimmed
1 lb (500 g) ground lamb
1 garlic clove, crushed
1 teaspoon ground cinnamon
2 teaspoons dried oregano
½ cup (150 ml) red wine or
  beef stock
One 13 oz (400 g) can chopped
  tomatoes
2 tablespoons tomato purée
1 lb (500 g) russet potatoes,
  peeled and ends trimmed
10 oz (300 g) plain Greek yogurt
2 eggs, beaten
4 oz (125 g) aged Cheddar cheese,
  shredded

This family meal is quick to prepare and contains a lot less fat than a traditional moussaka made with fried eggplant. Serve it with a crisp green salad for a well-rounded dinner.

Preheat the oven to 350°F (180°C).

Using a spiralizer fitted with a 3 mm (⅛ inch) spaghetti blade, spiralize the onion.

Place the ground lamb, spiralized onion and garlic in a large saucepan and dry-fry over medium-high heat for 3–4 minutes, until browned. Stir in the cinnamon, oregano, wine or stock, tomatoes and tomato purée, bring to a boil, then cover and simmer over low heat for 15 minutes.

Meanwhile, using a spiralizer fitted with a ribbon blade, spiralize the potatoes. Place the spiralized potatoes in a saucepan of lightly salted boiling water and simmer for 3–4 minutes, until just tender. Drain well.

In a small bowl, whisk together the yogurt and eggs until smooth and then stir in most of the cheese.

Place half of the lamb mixture in the bottom of a 1.5 litre (2½ pint) ovenproof dish. Cover with half the potatoes and then repeat the layers, finishing with a layer of potatoes. Spoon the yogurt mixture over the top of the potatoes and sprinkle with the remaining cheese.

Bake the moussaka for 25–30 minutes, until golden and bubbling. Serve with a crisp green salad.

spicy baked cod with potato topping

Serves 2
Prepare in 10 minutes
Bake in 40–45 minutes

1 yellow onion, ends trimmed

2 tablespoons sunflower oil

1 garlic clove, crushed

1 inch (2.5 cm) piece fresh ginger, peeled and chopped

2 tablespoons spicy or medium Indian-style curry paste

1 tablespoon lemon juice

One 13 oz (400 g) can chopped tomatoes

½ cup (150 ml) vegetable stock

Salt and freshly ground black pepper

7 oz (200 g) baby spinach

2 tablespoons chopped cilantro

2 russet potatoes, about 1 lb (500 g), peeled, ends trimmed and halved crosswise

2 thick pieces skinned cod, about 5–6 oz (150–175 g) each

Preheat the oven to 350°F (180°C).

Using a spiralizer fitted with a 3 mm (⅛ inch) spaghetti blade, spiralize the onion.

Heat 1 tablespoon of the oil in a large saucepan over medium heat and cook the spiralized onion, garlic and ginger for 2–3 minutes, until softened. Stir in the curry paste and cook for 1 minute. Add the lemon juice, tomatoes and stock and season with salt and pepper. Bring to a boil, then cover and simmer for 5 minutes. Stir in the spinach and cilantro and remove from the heat.

Using a spiralizer fitted with a 3 mm (⅛ inch) spaghetti blade, spiralize the potatoes. Place the spiralized potatoes on a clean dish towel and gently squeeze out any excess liquid. Pat the potatoes dry with paper towels.

Place the spiralized potatoes in a large bowl, add the remaining 1 tablespoon oil and season with salt and pepper. Stir to coat the potatoes in the oil and seasoning.

Pour the curry mixture into a 1-quart (1.2 litre) baking dish, arrange the cod pieces on top and cover the cod with the potatoes. Bake for 30–35 minutes or until the potatoes are crispy and tender and the cod is cooked through. Serve immediately.

butternut squash with ricotta and herbs

Serves 2
Prepare in 5 minutes
Cook in 10 minutes

½ butternut squash (the non-bulbous end), about 1 lb (500 g), peeled and halved crosswise

4 oz (125 g) ricotta cheese

2 tablespoons chopped fresh herbs, such as parsley, chives and basil

Finely grated zest and juice of 1 small organic lemon

1 tablespoon sunflower oil

1 garlic clove, crushed

3½ oz (100 g) baby spinach

3½ oz (100 g) frozen peas

¼ cup (2 fl oz) boiling water

Salt and freshly ground black pepper

Freshly grated Parmesan cheese

Using a spiralizer fitted with a 3 mm (⅛ inch) spaghetti blade, spiralize the squash.

In a small bowl, mix together the ricotta, herbs and lemon zest and juice to make a sauce.

Heat the oil in a large wok or frying pan over medium heat. Add the garlic and cook for 1 minute, then stir in the spiralized squash and stir-fry for about 5 minutes or until the squash starts to soften but is not breaking up. Stir in the spinach and peas and cook for 2 minutes, until the spinach has wilted.

Add the ricotta and herb sauce and the boiling water, stir and cook for another 1–2 minutes until the sauce has coated the squash. Season to taste with salt and pepper, sprinkle some Parmesan over the top and serve immediately.

Moroccan turkey burgers

Serves 6
Prepare in 10 minutes, plus chilling
Cook in 15 minutes

For the burgers
1 large zucchini, ends trimmed and
   halved crosswise
1 lb (500 g) lean ground turkey or
   chicken breast
4 green onions, chopped
1 garlic clove, crushed
2 tablespoons chopped mint
2 tablespoons chopped cilantro
1 tablespoon harissa paste
2 teaspoons ground cumin
1 egg, beaten
1 teaspoon salt
Freshly ground black pepper
1 tablespoon sunflower oil, for
   brushing

For the sumac-yogurt dip
7 oz (200 g) plain Greek yogurt
1 garlic clove, crushed
Grated zest and juice of ½ organic
   lemon
1 tablespoon sumac
Salt and freshly ground pepper to
   taste

These spiced burgers are delicious served with pita, lettuce leaves and large spoonfuls of sumac-yogurt dip.

Using a spiralizer fitted with a 3 mm (⅛ inch) spaghetti blade, spiralize the zucchini.

Place the ground turkey or chicken, green onions, garlic, mint, cilantro, harissa, cumin, egg, salt and pepper to taste in a large bowl and use your hands to mix the ingredients together. Divide the mixture into 6 portions and shape into large patties. Transfer the patties to a plate and chill in the refrigerator for 15 minutes. Preheat the broiler.

Place the patties on a nonstick baking sheet and brush the patties with a little oil. Cook the patties under the broiler for 6–7 minutes on each side or until cooked through.

While the burgers are cooking, make the dip. Place the yogurt, garlic, lemon zest and juice, and suman in a small bowl, mix together and season to taste.

Serve the burgers hot with the sumac-yogurt dip alongside.

zucchini spaghetti with sundried tomato pesto

Serves 4
Prepare in 10 minutes
Cook in 5 minutes

For the sundried tomato pesto
One 9½ oz (280 g) jar sundried
    tomatoes in olive oil
50 g (2 oz) pine nuts, lightly toasted
2 garlic cloves, chopped
1 teaspoon flaky sea salt
2 oz (50 g) basil leaves
4 oz (125 g) Parmesan cheese, grated

4 zucchini, ends trimmed and halved
    crosswise
2 tablespoons olive oil
Freshly ground black pepper
Arugula leaves, for serving

This recipe makes more sundried tomato pesto than you will need: the leftover pesto can be stored for 3–4 days in a jar or airtight container in the refrigerator. If you prefer to eat the zucchini spaghetti raw, just toss it in the pesto sauce and let it stand for 10 minutes to absorb the flavors.

First, make the sundried tomato pesto. Drain the sundried tomatoes, reserving the oil, and place them in a food processor with the pine nuts, garlic and salt. Process until a paste forms – you may need to scrape the mixture down the sides of the food processor with a rubber spatula from time to time. Add the basil leaves a few at a time and pulse until combined. Transfer to a bowl and stir in the Parmesan and the reserved tomato oil.

Using a spiralizer fitted with a 3 mm (⅛ inch) spaghetti blade, spiralize the zucchini.

Heat the oil in a large frying pan over medium heat and then gently sauté the zucchini for 2–3 minutes until heated through. Stir in half of the sundried tomato pesto and toss to coat the zucchini in the sauce.

Divide the zucchini among 4 bowls, season with plenty of pepper and serve with arugula leaves.

herbed sausage and bacon hash

Serves 2
Prepare in 5 minutes
Cook in 15–20 minutes

2 herbed pork sausages
1 yellow onion, ends trimmed
2 russet large potatoes, about 14½ oz
   (450 g) peeled, ends trimmed and
   halved crosswise
1 tablespoon sunflower oil
2 slices lean smoked bacon, chopped
Salt and freshly ground black pepper
2 eggs

Remove the sausage from the casings and break it into small pieces.

Using a spiralizer fitted with a 3 mm (⅛ inch) spaghetti blade, spiralize the onion and potatoes, keeping them separate. Place the spiralized potatoes on a clean dish towel and gently squeeze out any excess liquid.

Heat the oil in a frying pan over medium heat, add the sausage and bacon and cook for 3–4 minutes, stirring with a wooden spoon to break up the sausage, until the meat is brown and crispy. Add the spiralized onion and cook for 2 minutes or until softened, then stir in the potatoes and season with salt and pepper. Mix well and cook for 3–4 minutes, until starting to crisp. Turn over the mixture and cook for 3–4 minutes more, until the potatoes are crispy and cooked through.

Using the back of a spoon, make 2 deep wells in the mixture. Crack in the eggs and cook for 2–3 minutes or until the eggs are just set. Serve immediately.

plantain, chicken and coconut curry

Serves 4
Prepare in 10 minutes
Cook in 30 minutes

2 green plantains (the straightest
    ones you can find)
1 yellow onion, ends trimmed
2 tablespoons peanut oil
1 garlic clove, crushed
1 inch (2.5 cm) piece fresh ginger,
    grated
1 tablespoon medium spicy curry
    powder
3 boneless, skinless chicken breast
    halves, cut into chunks
14 fl oz (400 ml) coconut milk
1 cup (300 ml) chicken stock
Salt and freshly ground black pepper
Finely grated zest and juice of
    2 organic limes
7 oz (200 g) baby spinach

For serving
Naan bread
2 limes, halved

Cut the plantains in half crosswise. Score the outside of the skins and remove the skins, then trim the ends. Using a spiralizer fitted with a 3 mm (⅛ inch) spaghetti blade, spiralize the plantains. Spiralize the onion and keep separate from the plantain.

Heat 1 tablespoon of the oil in a large saucepan over medium heat, add the spiralized onion, garlic and ginger and cook gently for 3–4 minutes, until softened. Add the curry powder and cook for 1 minute, then stir in the chicken and cook for 3–4 minutes, until lightly browned. Stir in the coconut milk and stock, bring to a boil and then cover and simmer for 15 minutes. Season to taste with salt and pepper. Stir in most of the spiralized plantain, reserving a handful to fry later. Cover the pan and simmer for 5–6 minutes, until the plantains are just tender. Remove the saucepan from the heat. Stir in the lime zest and juice and the baby spinach, cover and let stand for 2–3 minutes, until the spinach is wilted.

Meanwhile, heat the remaining 1 tablespoon oil in a small frying pan over medium heat and cook the reserved spiralized plantain for 2–3 minutes, until crisp.

Spoon the curry into bowls and sprinkle with the crispy plantain. Serve immediately with naan bread and lime halves to squeeze over.

pork, apple and sage patties

Serves 4
Prepare in 5 minutes
Cook in 15 minutes

1 small yellow onion, ends trimmed
1 large apple, ends trimmed
1 lb (500 g) lean ground pork
2 tablespoons chopped sage
1 tablespoon grainy mustard
1 oz (25 g) dried bread crumbs
Salt and freshly ground black pepper
1 tablespoon sunflower oil
7 fl oz (200 ml) hot chicken stock

These pork patties also makes excellent burgers – just brush them with a little oil and then grill for 6–7 minutes on each side or until cooked through. Serve with sautéed or roasted seasonal vegetables to round out the meal.

Using a spiralizer fitted with a 3 mm (⅛ inch) spaghetti blade, spiralize the onion and apple.

Place the ground pork, spiralized onion and apple, sage, mustard and bread crumbs in a large bowl and season with salt and pepper. Mix well, using your hands, until all the ingredients are combined. Divide the mixture into 12 portions and shape into patties.

Heat the oil in a large frying pan over medium heat and then cook the patties for 3–4 minutes on each side, until cooked through. Remove the patties from the pan and set aside.

Pour the stock into the frying pan, bring to a simmer and cook for 2 minutes, stirring and scraping the browned bits from the bottom of the pan, until the liquid has reduced slightly.

Divide the patties among 4 plates and serve them with seasonal vegetables and the pan juices.

zucchini-crust Margherita pizza

Serves 4
Prepare in 10 minutes
Cook in 30 minutes

Sunflower oil, for brushing
4 zucchini, ends trimmed and halved
  crosswise
1 teaspoon garlic paste
4 oz (125 g) aged Cheddar cheese
2 teaspoons dried mixed herbs
2 oz (50 g) gluten-free all-purpose
  flour
2 eggs, beaten
1 teaspoon salt

For the tomato sauce
One 7 oz (200 g) can chopped
  tomatoes
2 tablespoons tomato purée
½ teaspoon superfine sugar
1 teaspoon dried Italian herbs

For the toppings
7 oz (200 g) mozzarella cheese, sliced
2 tomatoes, sliced
2 tablespoons prepared basil pesto
A few basil leaves

This pizza is suitable for those on a gluten-free diet. You can adapt the recipe by adding any of your favorite toppings.

Preheat the oven to 400°F (200°C).

Line a large baking sheet with nonstick baking paper and brush with a little oil.

Using a spiralizer fitted with a 3 mm (⅛ inch) spaghetti blade, spiralize the zucchini. Place the spiralized zucchini on a clean dish towel and gently squeeze out any excess liquid.

Transfer the zucchini to a large bowl, add the garlic paste, Cheddar, mixed herbs, flour, eggs and salt and mix well. Pour the mixture into the center of the prepared baking sheet and pat into a 12 inch (30 cm) round – this zucchini crust will form the base of the pizza.

Bake the crust for 20 minutes or until golden brown. Place a separate large baking sheet on top of the zucchini crust and, wearing oven mitts, carefully invert onto the new baking sheet. Peel off the parchment paper and return the zucchini crust to the oven for another 5 minutes, until golden.

Meanwhile, place the chopped tomatoes, tomato purée, sugar and dried herbs in a small saucepan and simmer over low heat for 5 minutes, stirring occasionally. Let cool slightly.

Spread the tomato sauce over the zucchini crust, arrange the mozzarella and tomatoes over the top and drizzle with the pesto. Return to the oven and bake for 5–6 minutes or until the cheese has melted. Scatter the basil leaves over the top and serve immediately.

spicy Mexican bean burgers

Serves 4
Prepare in 15 minutes, plus chilling
Cook in 15–20 minutes

1 yellow onion, ends trimmed
1 sweet potato, about 9 oz (275 g), peeled, ends trimmed and halved crosswise
1 tablespoon sunflower oil
1 green chile, seeded and finely chopped
2 teaspoons prepared Mexican or fajita spice mix
One 13 oz (400 g) can red kidney beans, drained and rinsed
4 tablespoons chopped cilantro
Salt and freshly ground black pepper
1 egg
2 teaspoons chipotle paste

For serving
4 flour tortillas, warmed
Crips green lettuce
Prepared fresh tomato salsa
Prepared guacamole
4 lime wedges

Using a spiralizer fitted with a 3 mm (⅛ inch) spaghetti blade, spiralize the onion and sweet potato.

Heat the oil in a small frying pan over medium heat and cook the spiralized onion and chile for 2–3 minutes, until softened. Stir in the spice mix and cook for 1 minute. Add the spiralized sweet potato and stir-fry for 4–5 minutes, until softened. Let cool slightly.

Mash the kidney beans in a large bowl with a potato masher or fork, then add the cilantro and season well with salt and pepper. Stir in the sweet potato mixture.

In a small bowl, beat together the egg and chipotle paste. Pour over the sweet potato and bean mixture and mix well with a fork. Using your hands, divide the mixture into 4 portions and shape into patties. Transfer the patties to a plate and chill in the refrigerator for 15 minutes. Preheat the broiler.

Place the patties on a nonstick baking sheet and broil for 4–5 minutes on each side, until golden and cooked through.

Top each tortilla with some lettuce, a spoonful of salsa and a burger and finish with a spoonful of guacamole. Serve with lime wedges to squeeze over.

beef and broccoli stir-fry

Serves 4
Prepare in 10 minutes, plus marinating
Cook in 10 minutes

2.5 cm (1 inch) piece fresh ginger, peeled and cut into thin strips

1 garlic clove, crushed

1 teaspoon cornstarch

2 tablespoons dark soy sauce

2 tablespoons dry sherry or Chinese cooking wine (Shaoxing)

1 lb (500 g) sirloin steak, trimmed of fat and cut into thin strips

2 carrots, peeled, ends trimmed and halved crosswise

1 head of broccoli, about 7 oz (200 g)

1 tablespoon sunflower oil

3 oz (75 g) cashews, toasted

10 oz (300 g) cooked egg noodles

2 tablespoons oyster sauce

3½ fl oz (100 ml) beef stock or water

Don't throw away broccoli stalks: spiralize them and add them to stir-fries instead.

In a large bowl, mix together the ginger, garlic, cornstarch and 1 tablespoon each of soy sauce and sherry or Chinese cooking wine. Stir in the steak and let marinate for 15 minutes.

Using a spiralizer fitted with a 3 mm (⅛ inch) spaghetti blade, spiralize the carrots. Change to a 6 mm (¼ inch) flat noodle blade, cut the broccoli stalk away from the florets and spiralize the stalk. Break the rest of the broccoli into small florets.

Bring a large saucepan of water to a boil and cook the broccoli florets for 2 minutes. Drain and plunge into cold water to stop the cooking. Drain again and pat dry with paper towels.

Heat 2 teaspoons of the oil in a wok or large frying pan over high heat until really hot. Add the beef strips with the marinade and stir-fry for 2–3 minutes, until the beef has browned. Remove the beef from the pan with a slotted spoon, transfer to a plate and set aside.

Add the remaining 1 teaspoon oil to the wok or frying pan. When the oil is hot, add the carrots, spiralized broccoli stalk, broccoli florets and cashews and cook for 2–3 minutes, until the vegetables are just tender.

Return the beef and any meat juices to the wok or frying pan. Add the noodles and stir in the remaining 1 tablespoon each of the soy sauce and sherry or Chinese cooking wine, the oyster sauce and stock or water. Cook, stirring constantly, until the sauce has coated all the ingredients. Serve immediately.

~smoked haddock~ cakes

Serves 4
Prepare in 20 minutes
Cook in 30–35 minutes

8 oz (250 g) skinless smoked
  haddock fillets
2 russet potatoes, about 14½ oz
  (450 g), peeled and ends trimmed
2 tablespoons chopped parsley
2 tablespoons mayonnaise
1 tablespoon grainy mustard
2 tablespoons all-purpose flour
1 egg, beaten
Salt and freshly ground black pepper

For serving
Arugula leaves
Lemon wedges

Preheat oven to 400°F (200°C).

Poach the smoked haddock in a saucepan of simmering water for 4–5 minutes or until the fish flakes easily. Remove the fish with a slotted spoon, transfer to a plate and let cool.

Using a spiralizer fitted with a 3 mm (⅛ inch) spaghetti blade, spiralize the potatoes. Place the spiralized potatoes in a saucepan of boiling water and simmer for 3–4 minutes, until just tender. Drain and allow to cool slightly.

Flake the fish into a large bowl. Add the potatoes, parsley, mayonnaise, mustard, flour and egg, mix well and season with salt and pepper.

Line a large baking sheet with parchment paper. Place a 3½ inch (8.5 cm) metal ring or cutter on the baking sheet and fill the ring or cutter with some of the fish mixture to form a thick cake. Remove the ring or cutter and repeat 7 more times to make 8 cakes total.

Bake the cakes for 20–25 minutes, until crispy. Serve the cakes with arugula leaves and lemon wedges to squeeze over.

sides
and extras

sweet potato dauphinoise

Serves 6
Prepare in 10 minutes
Bake in 1 hour

½ oz (15 g) butter
1 lb (500 g) russet potatoes, peeled,
   ends trimmed and halved crosswise
1 lb (500 g) sweet potatoes, peeled,
   ends trimmed and halved crosswise
1 large yellow onion, ends trimmed
2 garlic cloves, minced
2 tablespoons chopped rosemary
1½ cups (450 ml) milk
1 cup (300 ml) crème fraîche
Salt and freshly ground black pepper

Preheat the oven to 325°F (160°C).

Using a little of the butter, lightly grease a 6 cup (1.5 litre) baking dish. Using a spiralizer fitted with a ribbon blade, spiralize the potatoes and sweet potatoes, keeping them separate. Change to a 3 mm (⅛ inch) spaghetti blade and spiralize the onion.

Melt the remaining butter in a large saucepan over medium heat. Add the spiralized onion and cook for 3–4 minutes, until softened. Stir in the garlic and rosemary and cook for 1 minute. Stir in the milk and crème fraîche, season with salt and pepper and then stir in the spiralized potatoes. Bring to a simmer, then cover and cook over a low heat for 5 minutes. Stir in the spiralized sweet potatoes, cover and simmer for 3 minutes.

Transfer the mixture to the prepared dish, cover with foil and bake for 30 minutes. Uncover and cook for another 10 minutes or until the potatoes are tender.

spicy Asian coleslaw

Serves 4–6
Prepare in 10 minutes

1 cucumber, ends trimmed and cut
   into 3 pieces crosswise
1 large carrot, peeled, ends trimmed
   and cut into 3 pieces crosswise
1 daikon, about 8 oz (250 g), peeled,
   ends trimmed and halved crosswise

For the dressing
Finely grated zest and juice of
   2 organic limes
1 tablespoon rice wine vinegar
2 teaspoons grated fresh ginger
1 small red chile, seeded and
   chopped
1 teaspoon palm sugar or light brown
   sugar
1 teaspoon sesame oil

4 tablespoons chopped cilantro
2 tablespoons sesame seeds, lightly
   toasted

Using a spiralizer fitted with a 3 mm (⅛ inch) spaghetti blade, spiralize the cucumber and pat dry with paper towels. Using the same blade, spiralize the carrot and daikon.

To make the dressing, in a small bowl, mix together the lime zest and juice, vinegar, ginger, chile, sugar and sesame oil and stir until the sugar has dissolved.

Place the spiralized cucumber, carrot and daikon in a large bowl and sprinkle with the cilantro and sesame seeds. Pour in the dressing and toss well to coat all the ingredients. Chill the coleslaw in the refrigerator until ready to serve.

spiralized root vegetable rosti

Serves 4
Prepare in 10 minutes
Cook in 30–40 minutes

10 oz (300 g) russet potatoes, peeled
   and ends trimmed
5 oz (150 g) carrots, peeled, ends
   trimmed and halved crosswise
5 oz (150 g) parsnips, peeled, ends
   trimmed and halved crosswise
1 yellow onion, ends trimmed
1 tablespoon sunflower oil
2 teaspoons chopped thyme leaves
Salt and freshly ground black pepper

This is a great way to use up any assortment of root vegetables that are left in the refrigerator. A rosti (vegetable pancake) is a delicious accompaniment for roast meats or turn it into a main course by serving it with poached eggs.

Using a spiralizer fitted with a 3 mm (⅛ inch) spaghetti blade, spiralize all the vegetables, keeping the onion separate.

Place the spiralized potatoes, carrots and parsnips in a steamer over a pan of boiling water and steam for 5 minutes or until the potatoes are sticky and the carrots and parsnip are just tender.

Meanwhile, heat the oil in a 23 cm (9 inch) nonstick frying pan over medium heat and cook the spiralized onion for 2–3 minutes, until softened.

Stir in the steamed vegetables and thyme and season with salt and pepper. Cook for 4–5 minutes, without stirring, until the bottom of the vegetables starts to crisp. Turn over the vegetables, carefully pat them down with a large metal spatula and continue to cook for 4–5 minutes more. Repeat this process 2 more times or until the rosti is crispy and cooked through. Cut the rosti into wedges to serve.

mustardy celery root and potato gratin

Serves 6
Prepare in 10 minutes
Cook in 1 hour

2 tablespoons butter, plus extra for greasing
1 lb (500 g) russet potatoes, peeled and ends trimmed
13 oz (400 g) celery root, peeled and cut into 5 inch (12 cm) chunks
3 garlic cloves, crushed
Salt and freshly ground black pepper
1 cup (300 ml) heavy cream
1 cup (300 ml) milk
2 tablespoons grainy mustard

Preheat the oven to 325°F (160°C).

Grease a shallow 6 cup (1.5 litre) baking dish. Using a spiralizer fitted with a 6 mm (¼ inch) flat noodle blade, spiralize the potatoes and celery root, keeping them separate.

Place a handful of the spiralized potatoes in the base of the prepared dish, sprinkle with a little of the garlic and season with salt and pepper. Repeat, alternating layers of spiralized celery root and potato, until the dish is full.

Whisk the cream, milk and mustard together in a bowl and then pour over the vegetables. Dot the surface of the gratin with butter and bake for 1 hour, stirring halfway through the cooking time, until golden and tender.

crispy potato fries with rosemary and garlic

Serves 2–3
Prepare in 5 minutes
Cook in 10 minutes

2 large russet potatoes, peeled, ends
   trimmed and halved crosswise
3½ cups (1 litre) vegetable or
   sunflower oil, for deep frying
4 rosemary sprigs
8 garlic cloves, unpeeled
Flaky sea salt, for sprinkling

Using a spiralizer fitted with a 6 mm (¼ inch) flat noodle blade, spiralize the potatoes.

Heat the vegetable or sunflower oil in a wok or deep, heavy-based saucepan until it reads 350–375°F (180–190°C) on a deep-frying thermometer, or until a cube of bread dropped into the oil turns golden brown in 30 seconds.

Drop the rosemary and garlic into the hot oil and cook for 1 minute. Add the spiralized potatoes and deep-fry for 6–8 minutes, until golden brown and crispy. Remove from the oil with a slotted spoon and drain on paper towels. Sprinkle the fries with sea salt and serve immediately.

sides and extras   91

cucumber and mint raita

Serves 4
Prepare in 5 minutes

½ cucumber, ends trimmed and
    halved crosswise
7 fl oz (200 ml) plain yogurt
2 tablespoons chopped mint
½ teaspoon salt
½ teaspoon ground cumin

This cooling raita is really quick to make. It is the perfect accompaniment for spicy dishes such as Crispy Onion Bhajis (see page 24).

Using a spiralizer fitted with a 3 mm (⅛ inch) spaghetti blade, spiralize the cucumber. Dry the spiralized cucumber on paper towels.

Place the cucumber in a large bowl. Add the yogurt, mint, salt and cumin and mix well. Chill in the refrigerator until ready to serve.

beet, potato and chive rosti

Serves 4
Prepare in 10 minutes
Cook in 20 minutes

5 oz (150 g) russet potatoes, peeled
and ends trimmed
7 oz (200 g) golden beets, scrubbed
and ends trimmed
Salt and freshly ground black pepper
2 tablespoons chopped chives
2 tablespoons olive oil

Preheat the oven to 400°F (200°C).

Using a spiralizer fitted with a 3 mm (⅛ inch) spaghetti blade, spiralize the potatoes and beets. Place the spiralized vegetables on a clean dish towel and gently squeeze out any excess liquid.

Put the vegetables in a bowl, lightly season with salt and pepper, add the chives and drizzle with the oil. Using your hands, mix the vegetables to coat them with the oil, herbs and seasoning.

Place an 8.5 cm (3½ inch) metal ring or cutter on a large nonstick baking sheet and press a little of the rosti mixture into the ring or cutter to form a thin cake. Remove the ring or cutter and repeat 7 more times to make 8 rosti in total. (Alternatively, you can shape the rosti with your hands.)

Bake the rosti for 15 minutes, until crisp and golden. Carefully flip over the rosti and cook for another 5 minutes, until crisp.

apple and Calvados sauce

Serves 4
Prepare in 5 minutes
Cook in 10 minutes

3 Granny Smith apples, about 1½ lb
  (750 g), peeled and ends trimmed
Finely grated zest of ½ organic lemon
1 oz (25 g) superfine sugar
1 oz (25 g) butter
2 tablespoons Calvados

This unique applesauce is really easy to make and is delicious served with roast pork or duck. It will keep for about 1 week in the refrigerator and also freezes well.

Using a spiralizer fitted with a 6 mm (¼ inch) flat noodle blade, spiralize the apples.

Place the spiralized apples in a saucepan with the lemon zest, sugar, butter and Calvados and mix well. Cover and cook over low heat for 8–10 minutes, stirring occasionally, until the apples are soft. Let cool before serving.

spicy baked potato curls

Serves 4
Prepare in 5 minutes
Bake in 20 minutes

14½ oz (450 g) russet potatoes,
   peeled and ends trimmed
2 tablespoons sunflower oil
1 teaspoon garlic salt
2 teaspoons smoked paprika
1 teaspoon dried Italian herbs
Salt and freshly ground black pepper

Preheat the oven to 400°F (200°C).

Line a large baking sheet with parchment paper. Using a spiralizer fitted with a 6 mm (¼ inch) flat noodle blade, spiralize the potatoes.

Place the spiralized potatoes in a large bowl, add the oil, garlic salt, smoked paprika, dried herbs, and salt and pepper to taste and mix well to evenly coat the potatoes. Spread out the spiralized potatoes in a single layer on the prepared baking sheet.

Bake for 10 minutes, then stir the potato curls, moving the outside crispy ones to the center, and bake for another 10 minutes, until golden and crispy. Serve immediately.

celery root remoulade

Serves 4
Prepare in 10 minutes, plus standing

Juice of 1 lemon
4 heaped tablespoons mayonnaise
2 tablespoons crème fraîche
2 tablespoons Dijon mustard
2 tablespoons chopped parsley
Salt and freshly ground black pepper
1 small celery root, about 1 lb (500 g)

This creamy, crunchy vegetable salad is the perfect accompaniment for cold meats or smoked fish. The remoulade can be stored in the refrigerator for up to 2 days.

In a large bowl, mix together the lemon juice, mayonnaise, crème fraîche, mustard and parsley and season to taste with salt and pepper.

Using a sharp knife, remove the knobby peel from the celery root. Cut it in half crosswise and trim to make the ends flat. Using a spiralizer fitted with a 3 mm (⅛ inch) spaghetti blade, spiralize the celery root.

Immediately stir the spiralized celery root into the mayonnaise mixture, until evenly coated, and let stand for 30 minutes before serving.

spicy cucumber pickle

Serves 4

**Prepare in 10 minutes, plus
marinating**

1 cucumber, ends trimmed and cut
into 4 pieces crosswise
4 tablespoons rice wine vinegar
3 tablespoons superfine sugar
2 teaspoons salt
1 small red chile, seeded and finely
chopped
1 inch (2.5 cm) piece fresh ginger,
peeled and grated

*These pretty cucumber pickles are delicious served with
seared salmon or chicken. Keep any leftover pickles in the
refrigerator and use within a couple of days so that the
cucumber retains its crunch.*

Using a spiralizer fitted with a ribbon blade, spiralize the cucumber.
Dry the spiralized cucumber on paper towels and then place it in
a large bowl.

Whisk together the vinegar, sugar, salt, chile and ginger in a small
bowl and then pour over the cucumber. Gently toss to coat the
cucumber, cover and let marinate for at least 1 hour or overnight
in the refrigerator. To serve, drain the cucumber from the marinade.

Moroccan carrot salad

Serves 4
Prepare in 10 minutes, plus
marinating

14½ oz (450 g) large carrots, peeled
  and halved crosswise
2 tablespoons orange juice
1 tablespoon lemon juice
2 teaspoons orange blossom water
2 tablespoons extra-virgin olive oil
½ teaspoon ground cumin
½ teaspoon ground cinnamon
1 teaspoon confectioners' sugar
Flaky sea salt and freshly ground
  black pepper
1 preserved lemon, cut in half, pith
  and pulp removed and skin finely
  chopped
2 tablespoons chopped mint
Handful of mint leaves, for garnish

Carrots are usually grated for a Moroccan carrot salad,
but spiralizing them saves time and also retains the carrots'
lovely crunchy texture.

Using a spiralizer fitted with a 6 mm (¼ inch) flat noodle blade
or a ribbon blade, spiralize the carrots.

Combine the orange juice, lemon juice, orange blossom water, olive
oil, cumin, cinnamon and confectioners' sugar in a bowl and whisk
together. Season to taste with salt and pepper.

Add the spiralized carrots, preserved lemon and mint and lightly
toss. Place in the refrigerator and let marinate for 1–2 hours. Garnish
with the mint leaves just before serving.

roasted beets with balsamic glaze

Serves 4
Prepare in 5 minutes
Roast in 15–20 minutes

4 fresh beets, scrubbed and ends
    trimmed
1 tablespoon olive oil
3 tablespoons balsamic vinegar
Flaky sea salt and freshly ground
    black pepper

Roasted beets with balsamic vinegar are a perfect combination of flavors. This dish is great served as an accompaniment for meat or used in salads.

Preheat the oven to 375° F (190°C).

Using a spiralizer fitted with a 6 mm (¼ inch) flat noodle blade, spiralize the beets.

Place the spiralized beets in a roasting pan, drizzle with the oil and 2 tablespoons of the vinegar and season well with salt and pepper. Mix well.

Roast the beets for 15–20 minutes, turning halfway through the cooking time, until tender and slightly crispy. Stir in the remaining 1 tablespoon vinegar and let cool slightly before serving.

steamed vegetables with honey

Serves 4
Prepare in 5 minutes
Cook in 5 minutes

2 large carrots, peeled, ends trimmed
   and halved crosswise
3 zucchini, ends trimmed and
   halved crosswise
1 tablespoon honey
1 tablespoon lemon juice
½ teaspoon caraway seeds (optional)
Salt and freshly ground black pepper

Using a spiralizer fitted with a ribbon blade, spiralize the carrots and zucchini.

In a small bowl, mix together the honey, lemon juice and caraway seeds, if using.

Place the spiralized carrots in a steamer over a pan of boiling water and steam for 2 minutes. Add the spiralized zucchini and steam for a 3 minutes more or until the vegetables are just tender.

Transfer the steamed vegetables to a serving bowl, pour in the honey mixture and toss well. Season to taste with salt and pepper and serve immediately.

spiced turnip and pea fritters

Makes 12
Prepare in 10 minutes
Cook in 15–20 minutes

1 large turnip, about 1¼ lb (625 g), peeled and cut into 5 inch (12 cm) chunks

3 oz (75 g) chickpea flour

½ teaspoon ground turmeric

2 teaspoons garam masala

1 teaspoon cumin seeds

1 green chile, seeded and finely chopped

1 egg, beaten

3½ fl oz (100 ml) milk

1 teaspoon minced garlic

1 teaspoon minced ginger

2 tablespoons chopped cilantro

3½ oz (100 g) frozen peas, thawed

Salt and freshly ground black pepper

1 tablespoon peanut or sunflower oil, for frying

These spicy fritters are perfect for serving with grilled tandoori chicken or fish. They also make a great starter served with Cucumber and Mint Raita (see page 92) or mango chutney.

Using a spiralizer fitted with a 3 mm (⅛ inch) spaghetti blade, spiralize the turnip. Place the spiralized turnip in a steamer over a pan of simmering water and steam for 4 minutes, until just tender. Allow to cool slightly.

Meanwhile, in a large bowl, mix together the chickpea flour, spices and chile. Whisk together the egg, milk and garlic and ginger in a liquid measuring cup. Pour the egg mixture into the flour mixture and stir to make a thick batter. Stir in the cilantro and peas, season with salt and pepper and then stir in the turnip.

Heat a little oil in a large nonstick frying pan over medium heat. Cooking 4 fritters at a time, add heaped tablespoons of the batter to the pan, flatten slightly and cook for 2–3 minutes on each side, until crisp and brown. Repeat until all the batter is used up. Serve immediately.

crispy Parmesan and onion spirals

Serves 2–3
Prepare in 10 minutes
Cook in 10 minutes

2 large yellow onions, ends trimmed
2–3 tablespoons all-purpose flour
2 eggs
3½ oz (100 g) panko bread crumbs
2 oz (50 g) Parmesan cheese, grated
Salt and freshly ground black pepper
3½ cups (1 litre) vegetable or
    sunflower oil, for deep frying

Using a spiralizer fitted with a 6 mm (¼ inch) flat noodle blade, spiralize the onions.

Sprinkle the flour onto a plate. Beat the eggs together in a bowl. Mix together the bread crumbs and Parmesan in another bowl and season with salt and pepper.

Place the spiralized onions in the flour, toss to lightly coat and dust off any excess. Dip the onions in the egg mixture and then roll them in the Parmesan crumbs to coat.

Heat the vegetable or sunflower oil in a wok or deep, heavy-based saucepan until it reads 350–375°F (180–190°C) on a deep-frying thermometer, or until a cube of bread dropped into the oil turns golden brown in 30 seconds.

Carefully drop tablespoonfuls of the onion mixture into the hot oil, cooking about 4 at a time, and deep-fry the spirals for 2–3 minutes, until golden and crispy. Remove from the oil with a slotted spoon, drain on paper towels and keep warm while you cook the remaining mixture. Serve immediately.

sweet
treats

apple frangipane tart

Serves 8
Prepare in 15 minutes
Bake in 1 hour

Prepared dough for a 10-inch
   (25-cm) pie
3½ oz (100 g) unsalted butter
3½ oz (100 g) superfine sugar
2 large eggs
7 oz (200 g) ground almonds
½ teaspoon almond extract
1 tablespoon all-purpose flour, plus
   extra for dusting
2 large red apples, ends trimmed
1 oz (25 g) sliced almonds
2 tablespoons apricot preserves
   or jam
Whipped cream, for serving

Preheat oven to 350°F (180°C).

On a lightly floured work surface, roll out the dough until large enough to fit a 10-inch (25-cm) tart pan with a removable bottom. Line the pan with the dough. Prick the base with a fork, cover with parchment paper and fill with pie weights. Place the pan on a baking sheet and bake for 15 minutes. Remove the pie weights and parchment and return to the oven for 5 minutes, until golden.

In a large bowl, using an electric mixer on medium-high speed, cream together the butter and sugar until light and fluffy. Gradually beat in the eggs and then stir in the ground almonds, almond extract and flour. Spoon the mixture into the dough-lined pan.

Using a spiralizer fitted with a 6 mm (¼ inch) flat noodle blade, spiralize the apples.

Arrange the spiralized apples on top of the tart and sprinkle with the sliced almonds. Bake for 40–45 minutes, until golden and set.

Warm the apricot preserves or jam in a small saucepan and then brush over the top of the tart. Serve slices of the tart with spoonfuls of whipped cream.

beet and chocolate brownies

Makes about 24
Prepare in 15 minutes
Bake in 40 minutes

8 oz (250 g) unsalted butter, plus
    extra for greasing
9 oz (275 g) fresh beets, scrubbed
    and ends trimmed
8 oz (250 g) dark chocolate, chopped
3 eggs
9 oz (275 g) superfine sugar
1 teaspoon vanilla extract
3 oz (75 g) all-purpose flour
2 oz (50 g) unsweetened cocoa
    powder
Pinch of salt

Combining beets with chocolate was the original technique for making red velvet cake. In these rich brownies, the chocolate is the dominant flavor, while the beets lend nutrients and an earthy note. If you like, for a true red velvet experience, frost the brownies with the cream cheese frosting on page 110.

Preheat the oven to 350°F (180°C). Grease the bottom of an 8 inch (20 cm) square cake pan and line with parchment paper.

Using a spiralizer fitted with a 3 mm (⅛ inch) spaghetti blade, spiralize the beets. Place the spiralized beets in a saucepan and cover with cold water. Bring to a boil, then reduce the heat, cover and simmer for about 8 minutes or until tender. Drain well.

Place the beets in a food processor and process for a few minutes to form a smooth purée. Set aside.

Place the chocolate and butter in a heatproof bowl set over a saucepan of simmering water, taking care that the bowl does not actually touch the water. Heat until just melted, stirring occasionally, then remove from the heat and set aside.

In a large mixing bowl, whisk together the eggs, sugar and vanilla extract until pale and fluffy. Beat in the puréed beets and melted chocolate mixture. Sift in the flour, cocoa powder and salt and then fold them in until fully combined. Pour the batter into the prepared baking pan, smoothing the top with a spatula.

Bake for 30 minutes or until the center is almost set but still wobbles when you gently shake the pan. Remove from the oven and allow the cake to cool completely before carefully removing it from the pan. Peel off the parchment paper and cut the brownies into squares.

Asian pear fruit salad

Serves 4
Prepare in 5 minutes, plus cooling
Cook in 10 minutes

3½ oz (100 g) superfine sugar

2 lemongrass stalks, bruised and
 roughly chopped

1 inch (2.5 cm) piece fresh ginger,
 peeled and finely sliced

½ cup (150 ml) cold water

4 firm Asian pears (you can use
 regular pears or apples if you can't
 find Asian pears), ends trimmed

2 tablespoons chopped mint

3½ oz (100 g) pomegranate seeds

4 tablespoons shredded or flaked
 coconut

Place the sugar, lemongrass, ginger and water in a saucepan. Cook over low heat, stirring occasionally, until the sugar has dissolved. Bring the syrup to a boil, then reduce the heat and simmer for 5 minutes. Remove from the heat and let cool.

Once the syrup has cooled, use a spiralizer fitted with a ribbon blade to spiralize the pears – don't do this ahead of time or the pears will turn brown. Place the spiralized pears in a salad bowl.

Remove the lemongrass from the syrup and discard. Pour the syrup over the pears and then gently stir in the mint and pomegranate seeds. Chill in the refrigerator until ready to serve.

To serve, divide the salad among 4 bowls and sprinkle with the coconut.

carrot cake muffins

Makes 12
Prepare in 10 minutes
Bake in 18–20 minutes

1½ carrots, about 175 g (6 oz),
   peeled, ends trimmed and the
   whole carrot halved crosswise
6 oz (175 g) unsalted butter, softened
6 oz (175 g) superfine sugar
Grated zest of 1 organic orange plus
   1 tablespoon orange juice
6 oz (175 g) self-rising flour
2 teaspoons ground apple pie spice
2 eggs
2 oz (50 g) walnut pieces, chopped

For the frosting
7 oz (200 g) cream cheese
2 tablespoons confectioners' sugar
2 teaspoons grated orange zest
1 tablespoon orange juice

The spiralized carrots make these muffins deliciously moist. They are decorated with an orange and cream cheese frosting and spiralized carrot curls.

Preheat oven to 350°F (180°C).

Line a muffin pan with 12 paper muffin liners. Using a spiralizer fitted with a 3 mm (⅛ inch) spaghetti blade, spiralize the carrots.

In a large bowl, using an electric mixer on medium-high speed, beat together the butter, sugar and orange zest until pale and fluffy. Sift over the flour and spices, then add the eggs and orange juice and beat just until well combined. Stir in three-fourths of the spiralized carrots and the walnuts.

Divide the mixture among the muffin cases. Bake for 18–20 minutes, until risen and golden brown. Remove from the oven, place on a cooling rack and allow to cool.

To make the frosting, in a bowl, using an electric mixer on medium-high speed, beat together the cream cheese, confectioners' sugar, orange zest and juice until smooth. Spoon the frosting into a piping bag fitted with a star-shaped tip and pipe the frosting onto the cooled muffins. (Alternatively, you can spread the frosting over the top of the muffins with a knife.) Decorate the muffins with the remaining carrot curls.

stem ginger and apple cookies

Makes 12–14
Prepare in 15 minutes
Bake in 8–10 minutes

4 oz (125 g) rolled oats
3 oz (75 g) sunflower seeds
4 oz (125 g) self-rising flour
5 oz (150 g) unsalted butter,
  cut into cubes
2 tablespoons apple juice
5 oz (150 g) light brown sugar
3 tablespoons stem ginger syrup
1 large red apple, ends trimmed
3 pieces stem ginger, chopped

Look for stem ginger in syrup (chopped candied ginger packed with its cooking liquid) from a speciality food store or online source.

Preheat the oven to 325°F (160°C). Line 3 large baking sheets with parchment paper.

Mix together the oats, sunflower seeds and flour in a large bowl.

Place the butter in a saucepan with the apple juice, sugar and ginger syrup and cook over low heat, stirring with a wooden spoon, until the butter and sugar have melted.

Meanwhile, using a spiralizer fitted with a 3 mm (⅛ inch) spaghetti blade, spiralize the apple.

Pour the butter mixture over the dry ingredients in the bowl and mix together until combined. Gently fold in the spiralized apple and stem ginger.

Place heaped tablespoons of the mixture on each prepared baking sheet, leaving a fairly large space between each cookie to allow them to spread during cooking. Bake for 8–10 minutes, until golden. You may need to bake the cookies in batches.

Allow the cookies to cool on the baking sheets for a few minutes and then transfer them to a cooling rack with a spatula. Let them cool until they become crisp.

fall fruit salad

Serves 4
Prepare in 10 minutes, plus chilling

3 tablespoons pure maple syrup
½ teaspoon vanilla extract
1 teaspoon finely grated lemon zest
2 tablespoons lemon juice
¼ teaspoon ground cinnamon
2 firm pears, pointy ends trimmed
2 large red apples, ends trimmed
8 oz (250 g) blackberries
1 oz (25 g) pecans, chopped

This colourful autumnal dessert combines juicy blackberries with crisp apples and pears. Ideally, this fruit salad should be eaten on the day it is prepared.

In a large bowl, whisk together the maple syrup, vanilla extract, lemon zest and juice and cinnamon.

Using a spiralizer fitted with a ribbon blade, spiralize the pears and apples.

Place the spiralized pears and apples in the bowl with the syrup mixture and toss to coat in the syrup mixture. Stir in the blackberries. Chill in the refrigerator for about 30 minutes to allow the flavors to mingle.

Divide the fruit salad among 4 bowls, sprinkle with the pecans and serve immediately.

pear tarte tatin

Serves 4–6
Prepare in 10 minutes
Bake in 40 minutes

3 large firm pears, pointy ends
    trimmed
4 oz (125 g) superfine sugar
1½ oz (40 g) cold unsalted butter,
    cubed
½ teaspoon ground ginger
All-purpose flour, for dusting
12 oz (375 g) prepared, all-butter
    puff pastry
Heavy cream, for serving

You need to use firm pears for this recipe, otherwise the pears will release too much juice and make the pastry soggy.

Preheat the oven to 400°F (200°C).

Using a spiralizer fitted with a 6 mm (¼ inch) flat noodle blade, spiralize the pears.

Place an 8½ inch (21 cm) ovenproof frying pan over medium heat. Add the sugar and heat for 4–5 minutes, stirring constantly, until the sugar is a caramel color. Add the butter and ginger and stir to combine.

Place the spiralized pears in the frying pan and spoon caramel mixture over them until the pears are coated. Reduce the heat to medium-low and cook for 4–5 minutes, until the pears are slightly softened. Remove from the heat and let cool slightly.

On a lightly floured work surface, roll out the pastry to about ¼ inch (5 mm) thick. Cut a disk slightly bigger than your frying pan (about 24 cm/9½ inches in diameter). Place the pastry disk on top of the pears and then carefully tuck the pastry snugly around the outside of the pears and down into the sides of the pan.

Bake the tart for 30 minutes or until the pastry is golden brown and puffed up. Remove from the oven and let stand for 10 minutes.

Loosen the tart edges with a knife, place a large serving plate over the top and carefully invert the pan to turn the tart onto the plate. Cut into wedges and serve with heavy cream.

apple, raspberry and almond crumbles

Serves 4
Prepare in 10 minutes
Bake in 20–25 minutes

2 large or 3 red apples, ends trimmed
7 oz (200 g) fresh raspberries
2 tablespoons superfine sugar
4 tablespoons apple juice

For the topping
4 oz (125 g) all-purpose flour
3 oz (75 g) unsalted butter
4 tablespoons superfine sugar
4 tablespoons ground almonds

Vanilla ice cream, for serving

Preheat the oven to 375°F (190°C).

Using a spiralizer fitted with a 6 mm (¼ inch) flat noodle blade, spiralize the apples.

Place the spiralized apples in a large bowl and gently mix with the raspberries and sugar. Divide the mixture between four 8 fl oz (250 ml) ovenproof dishes and spoon 1 tablespoon of apple juice over the mixture in each dish.

Next, make the topping. In a large bowl, using your hands rub together the flour and butter until the mixture resembles fine bread crumbs (or pulse in a food processor to do this). Stir in the sugar and almonds.

Sprinkle the topping over the apple and raspberry mixture, dividing the topping among the 4 dishes. Bake for 20–25 minutes, until golden and bubbling. Serve with vanilla ice cream.

beet and blueberry pancakes

Serves 4
Prepare in 10 minutes
Bake in 10 minutes

1 fresh beet, scrubbed and ends
   trimmed
8 fl oz (250 ml) buttermilk
1 teaspoon vanilla extract
5 oz (150 g) buckwheat or all-
   purpose flour
½ teaspoon salt
2 teaspoons baking powder
1 tablespoon superfine sugar
1 egg
4 oz (125 g) blueberries
1 tablespoon sunflower oil

To serve
Plain Greek yogurt
Handful of blueberries
Pure maple syrup or honey

*These pancakes sound unusual but the beet gives them a
pretty pink color. In addition, their slightly earthy taste is
complemented by the sweet blueberries.*

Using a spiralizer fitted with a 3 mm (⅛ inch) spaghetti blade,
spiralize the beet.

Place the spiralized beet in a large jug with the buttermilk and vanilla
extract. Blend to form a smooth bright-red mixture.

Sift the flour, salt and baking powder into a large bowl and stir in the
sugar. Add the egg and then gradually beat the beet mixture into
the flour to make a smooth batter. Stir in the blueberries.

Heat a large nonstick frying pan over medium heat. Brush the pan
with oil. Drop 4 large tablespoons of the batter into the pan (this
will make 4 small pancakes) and cook for 2–3 minutes, until bubbles
start to appear on the surface and the underside is golden brown.
Flip over the pancakes and cook for another 2 minutes. Keep the
pancakes warm while you cook the remaining batter, greasing the
pan with a little more oil if necesssary.

Place 2 pancakes on each plate and serve with a dollop of yogurt,
some blueberries and a drizzle of maple syrup or honey.

sweet treats

apple, cinnamon and raisin muffins

Makes 10
Prepare in 10 minutes
Bake in 20–25 minutes

2 red apples, ends trimmed
9 oz (275 g) all-purpose flour
1 tablespoon baking powder
½ teaspoon salt
1 teaspoon ground cinnamon
4 oz (125 g) superfine sugar
1 egg
½ cup (150 ml) milk
3 fl oz (75 ml) sunflower oil
3 oz (75 g) golden raisins
2 tablespoons light brown sugar,
   for sprinking

Preheat the oven to 375°F (190°C).

Line a muffin pan with 10 paper muffin liners. Using a spiralizer fitted with a 6 mm (¼ inch) flat noodle blade, spiralize the apples.

In a large bowl, sift together the flour, baking powder, salt, cinnamon and superfine sugar.

In a large bowl with a spout, beat together the egg, milk and oil. Add the dry ingredients and mix until just combined. Stir in the spiralized apples and the raisins.

Divide the mixture among the muffin cups and then sprinkle the tops with brown sugar. Bake for 20–25 minutes, until risen and firm. Serve warm or at room temperature.

salted caramel and pear pudding

Serves 4
Prepare in 15 minutes
Bake in 35–40 minutes

3½ oz (100 g) unsalted butter,
    melted, plus extra for greasing
4 firm baking pears, pointy ends
    trimmed
4 oz (125 g) all-purpose flour
2 teaspoons baking powder
4 oz (125 g) superfine sugar
7 fl oz (200 ml) milk
1 egg, beaten
5 oz (150 g) light brown
    muscovado sugar
4 tablespoons golden syrup
2 teaspoon flaky sea salt
8 fl oz (250 ml) water
Vanilla ice cream, for serving

This easy-to-make dessert combines juicy pears with a sticky salted caramel sauce and a light sponge cake. It is delicious served with vanilla ice cream. Golden syrup is a light brown syrup made from cane sugar and popular in British-style recipes. Seek it out from an online source.

Preheat the oven to 350°F (180°C).

Grease a 5 cup (1.5 litre) baking dish. Using a spiralizer fitted with a 6 mm (¼ inch) flat noodle blade, spiralize the pears. Place the spiralized pears in the prepared dish.

Sift the flour and baking powder into a large bowl. Add the superfine sugar, milk, melted butter and egg and whisk together for 2–3 minutes until well combined. Pour the mixture over the pears.

To make the salted caramel sauce, place the brown sugar, golden syrup and salt in a small saucepan and add the water. Cook over medium-high heat, stirring until the sugar has dissolved, then bring to a boil.

Carefully pour the sauce over the pudding and bake for 30–35 minutes, until the pudding is set. Allow the pudding to stand for 5 minutes, then serve portions with vanilla ice cream.

zucchini and lemon drizzle cake

Serves 8
Prepare in 20 minutes
Bake in 40–45 minutes

7 oz (200 g) unsalted butter,
  softened, plus extra for greasing
2 zucchini, ends trimmed and halved
  crosswise
Finely grated zest of 2 organic lemons
7 oz (200 g) superfine sugar
3 eggs, beaten
7 oz (200 g) self-rising flour, sifted

For the lemon syrup
3 oz (75 g) granulated sugar
Juice of 2 lemons (about 100 ml/
  3½ fl oz)

Handful of Candied Lemon Peel
  (see page 124), for decorating

The spiralized zucchini add moisture to this intensely lemony cake. The cake's crusty topping is made by pouring lemon syrup over the top while the cake is still warm.

Preheat the oven to 350°F (180°C). Grease an 8 inch (20 cm) springform pan and line the base with parchment paper.

Using a spiralizer fitted with a ¼ inch (3 mm) spaghetti blade, spiralize the zucchini. Roughly snip any really long spirals in half with scissors.

Place the lemon zest, butter and sugar in a mixing bowl and beat with an electric mixer on medium-high speed until light and fluffy. Add the eggs a little at a time, beating well after each addition. If the mixture starts to curdle, add 1 tablespoon of the flour. Using a metal spoon, fold in the spiralized zucchini and flour until you have a really thick mixture.

Spoon the mixture into the prepared pan and bake in the center of the oven for 40–45 minutes, until risen, golden and shrinking away from the sides of the pan.

Meanwhile, as soon as the cake goes into the oven, make the lemon syrup. Put the sugar and lemon juice in a small bowl and set in a warm place (next to the oven is ideal) while the cake bakes, stirring the mixture occasionally.

Remove the cake from the oven and prick all over the surface of the cake, about 20 times, with a skewer. Slowly drizzle the lemon syrup over the cake, waiting a few moments for the syrup to sink in before adding more. Let the cake cool in the pan for 10 minutes, then remove from the pan and transfer to a cooling rack to cool completely. Decorate with the candied lemon peel.

candied lemon peel

Makes enough to decorate 2 large cakes
Prepare in 5 minutes, plus cooling
Cook in 10 minutes

4 large organic lemons
3½ oz (100 g) superfine sugar, plus about 2 tablespoons for sprinkling
3½ fl oz (100 ml) cold water

Spiralizing lemon peel is so much quicker than using a knife to cut strips of peel and it results in much prettier spirals. Use this candied peel to decorate cakes such as the Zucchini and Lemon Drizzle Cake on page 122.

Cut the lemons in half crosswise and squeeze out the juice. (The juice isn't needed for this recipe so store it in the refrigerator to be used another time.) Secure the uncut end of one of the lemon halves to a spiralizer fitted with a ribbon blade and spiralize into strips. Repeat with the remaining lemon halves. Remove and discard any of the pith that has separated from the lemon peel.

Place the sugar and water in a small saucepan and bring to a boil, stirring continuously. Add the spiralized lemon peel and boil for 4–5 minutes or until syrupy and the peel is translucent.

Line a baking sheet with parchment paper. Spread out the peel in a single layer on the prepared baking sheet and separate the lemon peel spirals with a fork. Sprinkle the remaining sugar over the spirals and then roll them in the sugar to coat thoroughly.

Let the peel dry in a warm place for a couple of hours, or overnight if possible. The candied peel can be stored for up to 3 weeks in an airtight container.

gooey chocolate and pear puddings

Serves 4
Prepare in 10 minutes
Bake in 20 minutes

5 oz (150 g) unsalted butter,
   softened, plus extra for greasing
2 small firm pears, pointy ends
   trimmed
7 oz (200 g) light brown sugar
1 teaspoon vanilla extract
4 oz (125 g) self-rising flour, sifted
2 oz (50 g) unsweetened cocoa
   powder, sifted
2 eggs
Heavy cream or crème fraîche,
   for serving

Preheat the oven to 350°F (180°C).

Grease four ½-cup (150-ml) ramekins and line the bases with parchment paper. Using a spiralizer fitted with a 3 mm (⅛ inch) spaghetti blade, spiralize the pears.

Place the butter, sugar and vanilla extract in a large bowl and beat with an electric mixer on medium-high speed until light and fluffy. Add the flour, cocoa powder and eggs and beat just until combined. Stir in the spiralized pears.

Divide the mixture between the prepared ramekins. Place the ramekins on a baking sheet and bake for 20 minutes, or until almost set but still slightly soft in the middle.

Invert the puddings onto plates, remove the parchment paper and serve immediately with heavy cream or crème fraîche.

index

almonds
apple frangipane tart 106
apple, raspberry and almond
crumbles 116
apples 6
apple and Calvados
sauce 94
apple, endive and walnut
salad 44
apple, cinnamon and raisin
muffins 119
apple frangipane tart 106
apple, raspberry and almond
crumbles 116
baked apple and cinnamon
chips 18
candied ginger and apple
cookies 112
pork, apple and sage patties
76
Asian coleslaw, spicy 87
Asian pear fruit salad 109

bacon
herbed sausage and bacon
hash 73
Jerusalem artichoke and
bacon salad 40
balsamic glaze, roasted beets
with 100
bean burgers, spicy Mexican
78
beef
beef and broccoli stir-fry
81
cottage pie with crispy
topping 54
Thai beef salad 38
beets 6
baked vegetable chips 30
beet and blueberry
pancakes 118
beet and chocolate
brownies 108
beet, potato and chive
rosti 93
beet, smoked trout and
horseradish salad 49
roasted beets with
balsamic glaze 100
bhajis, crispy onion 24
blueberries: beet and blueberry
pancakes 118
borlotti beans: fall vegetable
minestrone 27

bread: zucchini and haloumi
bruschetta 17
broccoli 6
beef and broccoli stir-fry 81
brownies, beet and chocolate
108
bruschetta, zucchini and
haloumi 17
burgers
spicy Mexican bean burgers
78
Moroccan turkey burgers 70
butternut squash 6
butternut squash, feta and
Puy lentil salad 37
butternut squash, sage and
goat cheese tart 52
butternut squash with ricotta
and herbs 69
butternut squash with sage
and pine nuts 59
squash, cheese and chive
muffins 29

cakes
beet and chocolate
brownies 108
carrot cake muffins 110
zucchini and lemon drizzle
cake 122
Calvados: apple and Calvados
sauce 94
candied lemon peel 124
caramel: salted caramel and
pear pudding 121
carrots 6
carrot cake muffins 110
daikon, carrot and cucumber
laksa 16
Moroccan carrot salad 98
shepherd's pie with crispy
topping 54
Thai beef salad 38
celery root 6–7
celery root remoulade 96
fall vegetable minestrone 27
mustardy celery root and
potato gratin 90
cheese
butternut squash, feta and
Puy lentil salad 37
butternut squash, sage and
goat cheese tart 52
butternut squash with ricotta
and herbs 69

crispy Parmesan and onion
spirals 103
easy potato moussaka 66
Greek salad pita pockets 19
pear, ham and blue cheese
salad 47
pumpkin, cheese and chive
muffins 29
zucchini and haloumi
bruschetta 17
zucchini-crust Margherita
pizza 77
zucchini, feta and mint
fritters 13
see also ricotta cheese
chicken
baked chicken with sweet
potatoes 56
chicken, zucchini and
quinoa salad 34
green papaya and chicken
salad 45
plantain, chicken and
coconut curry 74
Vietnamese chicken and
noodle salad 44
chiles: zucchini with crab, chile
and lemon 55
chips
baked apple and cinnamon
chips 18
baked vegetable chips 30
salt and vinegar baked
potato chips 22
chives: beet, potato and chive
rosti 93
chocolate
beet and chocolate
brownies 108
gooey chocolate and pear
puddings 125
chorizo
Mexican baked potato nests
14
Spanish chorizo tortilla 63
chowder, smoked haddock 28
coconut cream: curried sweet
potato puffs 58
coconut milk: plantain, chicken
and coconut curry 74
cod: spicy baked cod with
potato topping 67
coleslaw, spicy Asian 86
cookies, candied ginger and
apple 112

crab
crab and vegetable dim
sum 23
zucchini with crab, chile and
lemon 55
crumble, apple, raspberry and
almond 116
cucumber 7
cucumber and mint raita 92
daikon, carrot and cucumber
laksa 16
Greek salad pita pockets 19
spicy cucumber pickles 97
curry
curried sweet potato puffs 58
plantain, chicken and
coconut curry 74

daikon 7
daikon, carrot and cucumber
laksa 16
shrimp pad Thai 60
shrimp rice paper wraps 12
spicy Asian coleslaw 86
Thai beef salad 38
Japanese tuna tataki salad 36
dauphinoise, sweet potato 86
dill: smoked salmon salad with
dill and lemon 41
dim sum, crab and vegetable
23
dip, sumac-yogurt 70

edamame beans: vegetable
noodle miso soup 10
eggs
Mexican baked potato nests
14
mini sweet potato and
ricotta frittatas 20
shrimp pad Thai 60
smoked mackerel with
quail egg salad 42
Spanish chorizo tortilla 63
endive: apple, endive and
walnut salad 44

fall
fall fruit salad 113
fall vegetable minestrone 27
fish
beet, smoked trout and
horseradish salad 49
Japanese tuna tataki salad
36

sesame and ginger salmon en papilotte 64
smoked haddock chowder 28
smoked haddock cakes 82
smoked mackerel with quail egg salad 42
smoked salmon salad with dill and lemon 41
spicy baked cod with potato topping 67
frangipane: apple frangipane tart 106
fries: crispy potato fries with rosemary and garlic 91
frittatas, mini sweet potato and ricotta 20
fritters
  spiced parsnip and pea fritters 102
  zucchini, feta and mint fritters 13
fruit
  Asian pear fruit salad 109
  fall fruit salad 113
  which fruit to spiralize 6–7
  see also apples; pears, etc

garlic, crispy potato fries with rosemary and 91
ginger
  candied ginger and apple cookies 112
  sesame and ginger salmon en papilotte 64
goat cheese: butternut squash, sage and goat cheese tart 52
gooey chocolate and pear puddings 125
gratin, mustardy celery root and potato 90
Greek salad pita pockets 19
green papaya 7
  green papaya and chicken salad 45

haddock
  smoked haddock chowder 28
  smoked haddock cakes 82
haloumi: zucchini and haloumi bruschetta 17
ham: pear, ham and blue cheese salad 47
herbs
  butternut squash with ricotta and herbs 69
  herbed sausage and bacon hash 73
honey, steamed vegetables with 101
horseradish: beet, smoked trout and horseradish salad 49

Japanese tuna tataki salad 36
Jerusalem artichokes 7
  Jerusalem artichoke and bacon salad 40

laksa, daikon, carrot and cucumber 16
lamb: easy potato moussaka 66
lemons
  candied lemon peel 124
  smoked salmon salad with dill and lemon 41
  zucchini and lemon drizzle cake 122
  zucchini with crab, chile and lemon 55
lentils: butternut squash, feta and Puy lentil salad 37

mackerel: smoked mackerel with quail egg salad 42
mayonnaise: celery root remoulade 96
Mexican baked potato nests 14
Mexican, spicy bean burgers 78
minestrone, fall vegetable 27
mint
  cucumber and mint raita 92
  zucchini, feta and mint fritters 13
  miso soup, vegetable noodle 10
Moroccan carrot salad 98
Moroccan turkey burgers 70
moussaka, easy potato 66
muffins
  apple, cinnamon and raisin muffins 119
  carrot cake muffins 110
  pumpkin, cheese and chive muffins 29
mustardy celeriac and potato gratin 90

noodles
  beef and broccoli stir-fry 81
  Vietnamese chicken and noodle salad 46

oats: candied ginger and apple cookies 112
olives: Greek salad pita pockets 19
onions 7
  crispy onion bhajis 24
  crispy Parmesan and onion spirals 103

pad Thai, shrimp 60
pancakes, beet and blueberry 118

pancetta: fall vegetable minestrone 27
parsnips 7
  baked vegetable chips 30
  spiralized root vegetable rosti 88
pastry puffs, curried sweet potato 58
patties, pork, apple and sage 76
pears 7
  gooey chocolate and pear puddings 125
  pear, ham and blue cheese salad 47
  pear tarte tatin 114
  salted caramel and pear pudding 121
peas
  butternut squash with ricotta and herbs 69
  spiced parsnip and pea fritters 102
pesto, sundried tomato 72
pickles, spicy cucumber 97
pine nuts, butternut squash with sage and 59
pita pockets, Greek salad 19
pizza, zucchini-crust Margherita 77
plantains 7
  plantain, chicken and coconut curry 74
pomegranate seeds
  Asian pear fruit salad 109
  chicken, zucchini and quinoa salad 34
pork, apple and sage patties 76
potatoes 7
  beet, potato and chive rosti 93
  crispy potato fries with rosemary and garlic 91
  crispy potato straws 42
  easy potato moussaka 66
  herbed sausage and bacon hash 73
  Mexican baked potato nests 14
  mustardy celery root and potato gratin 90
  salt and vinegar baked potato chips 22
  smoked haddock chowder 28
  smoked haddock cakes 82
  Spanish chorizo tortilla 63
  spicy baked cod with potato topping 67
  spicy potato curls 95
  spiralized root vegetable rosti 88

sweet potato dauphinoise 86
pumpkin, cheese and chive muffins 29

quail eggs: smoked mackerel with quail egg salad 42
quinoa: chicken, zucchini and quinoa salad 34

raisins: apple, cinnamon and raisin muffins 119
raita, cucumber and mint 92
raspberries: apple, raspberry and almond crumbles 116
red kidney beans: spicy Mexican bean burgers 78
remoulade, celery root 96
rice noodles: Vietnamese chicken and noodle salad 46
rice paper wraps, shrimp 12
ricotta cheese
  butternut squash with ricotta and herbs 69
  mini sweet potato and ricotta frittatas 20
rosemary: crispy potato fries with rosemary and garlic 91
rosti
  beet, potato and chive rosti 93
  spiralized root vegetable rosti 88

sage
  butternut squash, sage and goat cheese tart 52
  butternut squash with sage and pine nuts 59
  pork, apple and sage patties 76
salads 32–49
  apple, endive and walnut salad 44
  Asian pear fruit salad 109
  beet, smoked trout and horseradish salad 49
  butternut squash, feta and Puy lentil salad 37
  chicken, zucchini and quinoa salad 34
  fall fruit salad 113
  Greek salad pita pockets 19
  green papaya and chicken salad 45
  Japanese tuna tataki salad 36
  Jerusalem artichoke and bacon salad 40
  Moroccan carrot salad 98
  pear, ham and blue cheese salad 47
  smoked mackerel with quail egg salad 42

index

smoked salmon salad with dill and lemon 41
spicy Asian coleslaw 86
Thai beef salad 38
Vietnamese chicken and noodle salad 46
salmon
  sesame and ginger salmon en papillote 64
  smoked salmon salad with dill and lemon 41
salt and vinegar baked potato chips 22
salted caramel and pear pudding 121
sauce, apple and Calvados 94
sausages: herbed sausage and bacon hash 73
sesame and ginger salmon en papillote 64
shepherd's pie with crispy topping 54
shrimp
  shrimp pad Thai 60
  shrimp rice paper wraps 12
smoked haddock
  smoked haddock chowder 28
  smoked haddock cakes 82
smoked mackerel with quail egg salad 42
smoked salmon salad with dill and lemon 41
smoked trout: beet, smoked trout and horseradish salad 49

soups
  daikon, carrot and cucumber laksa 16
  fall vegetable minestrone 27
Spanish chorizo tortilla 63
spinach
  butternut squash with ricotta and herbs 69
  plantain, chicken and coconut curry 74
  spicy baked cod with potato topping 67
spiral vegetable tempura 26
spiralized root vegetable rosti 88
spiralizers, introduction to 4–6
stir-fry, beef and broccoli 81
storing spiralized vegetables 7
sumac-yogurt dip 70
sundried tomato pesto 72
sweet potatoes 7
  baked vegetable crisps 30
  chicken traybake with sweet potatoes 56
  curried sweet potato puffs 58
  mini sweet potato and ricotta frittatas 20
  spicy Mexican bean burgers 78
  sweet potato dauphinoise 86

tarts
  apple frangipane tart 106
  butternut squash, sage and goat cheese tart 52

pear tarte tatin 114
tempura, spiral vegetable 26
Thai beef salad 38
tomatoes
  easy potato moussaka 66
  Greek salad pita pockets 19
  sundried tomato pesto 72
  zucchini-crust Margherita pizza 77
tortilla, Spanish chorizo 63
trout: beet, smoked trout and horseradish salad 49
tuna: Japanese tuna tataki salad 36
turkey burgers, Moroccan 70
turnips 7
  spiced turnip and pea fritters 102

vegetables
  baked vegetable chips 30
  cooking and storing 7
  crab and vegetable dim sum 23
  spiral vegetable tempura 26
  spiralized root vegetable rosti 88
  steamed vegetables with honey 101
  vegetable noodle miso soup 10
  which vegetables to use 6–7
  see also carrots; potatoes, etc
Vietnamese chicken and noodle salad 46

walnuts: apple, endive and walnut salad 44

yogurt
  cucumber and mint raita 92
  easy potato moussaka 66
  sumac-yogurt dip 70

zucchini 7
  chicken, zucchini and quinoa salad 34
  zucchini and haloumi bruschetta 17
  zucchini and lemon drizzle cake 122
  zucchini-crust Margherita pizza 77
  zucchini, feta and mint fritters 13
  zucchini with crab, chile and lemon 55
  zucchini with sundried tomato pesto 72

acknowledgments

Photographer: William Shaw
Food Stylist: Denise Smart
Prop Stylist: Kim Sullivan